Take It to Your Seat Centers

Reading & Language
5

Using the Centers

The centers in this book are intended for skill practice and reinforcement, not as an introduction to skills. It is important to model the use of each center before students are asked to do the tasks independently.

Why Use Centers?

- Centers are a motivating way for students to practice important skills.

- They appeal especially to kinesthetic and visual learners.

- The 12 centers in this book are self-contained and portable. Students can work at a desk, at a table, or on a rug.

- Once you've made the centers, they're ready to use at any time.

Before Using Centers

You and your students will enjoy using the centers more if you think through logistical considerations. Here are a few questions to resolve ahead of time:

- Will students select a center, or will you assign the centers and use them as a skill assessment tool?

- Will there be a specific block of time for centers, or will the centers be used throughout the day as students complete other work?

- Where will you place the centers for easy access by students?

- What procedure will students use when they need help with the center tasks?

- Will students use the answer key to check their own work?

- How will you use the center checklist to track student completion of the centers?

A Place for Centers

Make the centers ahead of time so that they are ready for student use whenever specific skill practice is indicated.

Store the prepared centers in a filing box or crate. If you wish the centers to be self-checking, include the answer key with the center materials.

Introducing the Centers

Use the student direction cover page to review the skill to be practiced.

Read each step to the students and model what to do, showing students the center pieces.

Record Progress

Use the center checklist (page 4) to record the date and student achievement.

Making the Centers

Included in Each Center

(A) Student direction cover page

(B) Task cards and/or mats

(C) Reproducible student response form

(D) Answer key

Materials Needed

- Colored file folders with inside pockets
- Small envelopes or plastic self-closing bags (for storing cut task cards)
- Pencils and marking pens (for labeling envelopes)
- Scissors
- Double-sided tape
- Laminated center pieces
- Answer key pages

Steps to Follow

1. Tape the student direction page to the front of the file folder.

2. Place the reproduced response forms in the left-hand pocket.

3. Laminate the task cards and mats. Put the cut cards in a labeled envelope or plastic self-closing bag. Place the mats and task cards in the right-hand pocket of the file folder.

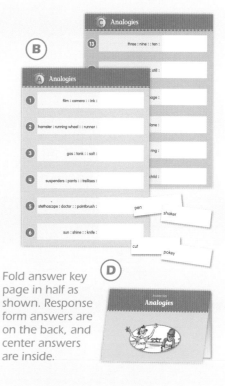

Fold answer key page in half as shown. Response form answers are on the back, and center answers are inside.

Assembled Center

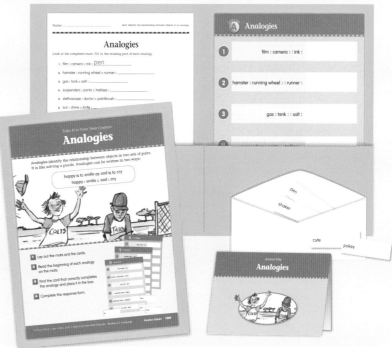

Student _____

Center Checklist

Center / Skills	Skill Level	Date
1. Idioms Recognize idioms as phrases that mean something different from what the individual words seem to mean		
2. Synonyms/Antonyms Distinguish if a pair of words are synonyms or antonyms		
3. Homophones Identify homophones as words that sound alike but have different spellings and meanings		
4. Homographs Identify homographs as words that sound and are spelled the same but have different meanings		
5. Prefixes Identify prefixes as word parts added to the beginning of a word which change the meaning of that word		
6. Suffixes Identify suffixes as word parts added to the end of a word which change the meaning and part of speech of that word		
7. Greek and Latin Roots Identify word roots that form the base of words and can give clues to the words' meanings		
8. Parts of Speech Identify proper nouns, past tense verbs, descriptive adjectives, adverbs, pronouns, and prepositions		
9. Analogies Identify the relationship between objects in an analogy		
10. Fact or Opinion? Determine the difference between fact and opinion in written text		
11. Word Meaning from Context Use context clues when reading to determine the meaning of unfamiliar words in written text		
12. Main Idea Identify the main idea of a paragraph and choose the best title		

Idioms

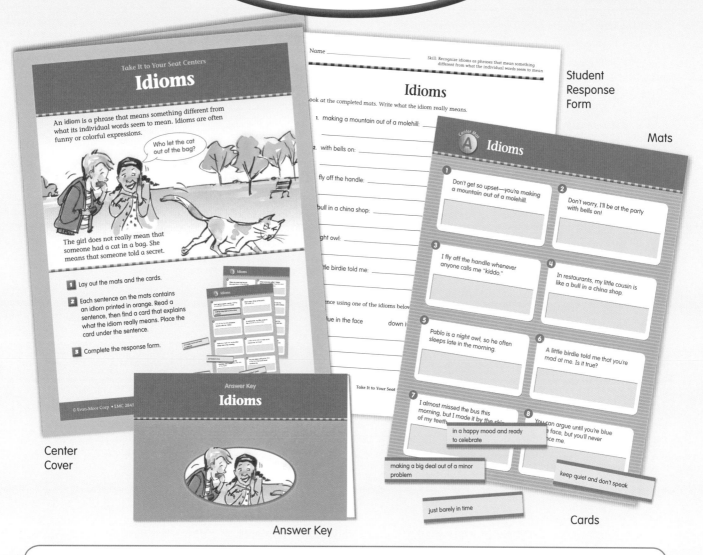

Student Response Form

Mats

Center Cover

Answer Key

Cards

Skill
Recognize idioms as phrases that mean something different from what the individual words seem to mean

Prepare the Center
Follow the directions on page 3.

Introduce the Center
Demonstrate how to use the center. State the goal: *You will read each sentence containing a highlighted idiom, then place a card on the mat to show the meaning of the idiom.*

Idioms

Look at the completed mats. Write what the idiom really means.

1. making a mountain out of a molehill: _____

   _____

2. with bells on: _____

   _____

3. fly off the handle: _____

   _____

4. bull in a china shop: _____

   _____

5. night owl: _____

   _____

6. A little birdie told me: _____

   _____

Write a sentence using one of the idioms below.

        blue in the face   down in the dumps   button his lip

_____

_____

_____

Take It to Your Seat Centers—Reading & Language • EMC 2845 • © Evan-Moor Corp.

Idioms

An **idiom** is a phrase that means something different from what its individual words seem to mean. Idioms are often funny or colorful expressions.

Who **let the cat out of the bag**?

The girl does not really mean that someone had a cat in a bag. She means that someone told a secret.

1 Lay out the mats and the cards.

2 Each sentence on the mats contains an idiom printed in orange. Read a sentence, then find a card that explains what the idiom really means. Place the card under the sentence.

3 Complete the response form.

Idioms

Answer Key

(fold)

Response Form

Idioms

Look at the completed mats. Write what the idiom really means.

1. making a mountain out of a molehill: making a big deal out of a minor problem

2. with bells on: in a happy mood and ready to celebrate

3. fly off the handle: get very angry

4. bull in a china shop: a person who is extremely clumsy

5. night owl: a person who likes to stay up late

6. A little birdie told me: I was told by someone whose name I won't mention

Write a sentence using one of the idioms below.

| blue in the face | down in the dumps | button his lip |

Answers will vary.

Answer Key

Idioms

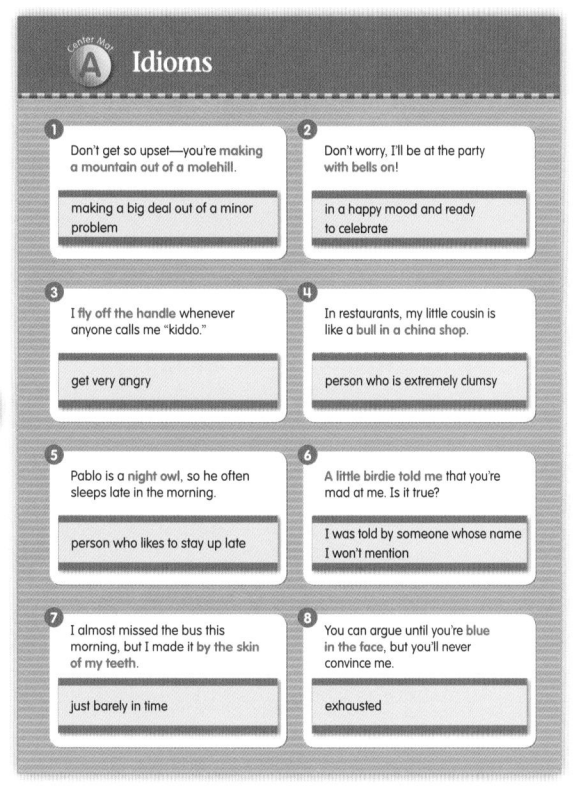

A Idioms

1 Don't get so upset—you're making a mountain out of a molehill.

making a big deal out of a minor problem

2 Don't worry, I'll be at the party with bells on!

in a happy mood and ready to celebrate

3 I fly off the handle whenever anyone calls me "kiddo."

get very angry

4 In restaurants, my little cousin is like a bull in a china shop.

person who is extremely clumsy

5 Pablo is a night owl, so he often sleeps late in the morning.

person who likes to stay up late

6 A little birdie told me that you're mad at me. Is it true?

I was told by someone whose name I won't mention

7 I almost missed the bus this morning, but I made it by the skin of my teeth.

just barely in time

8 You can argue until you're blue in the face, but you'll never convince me.

exhausted

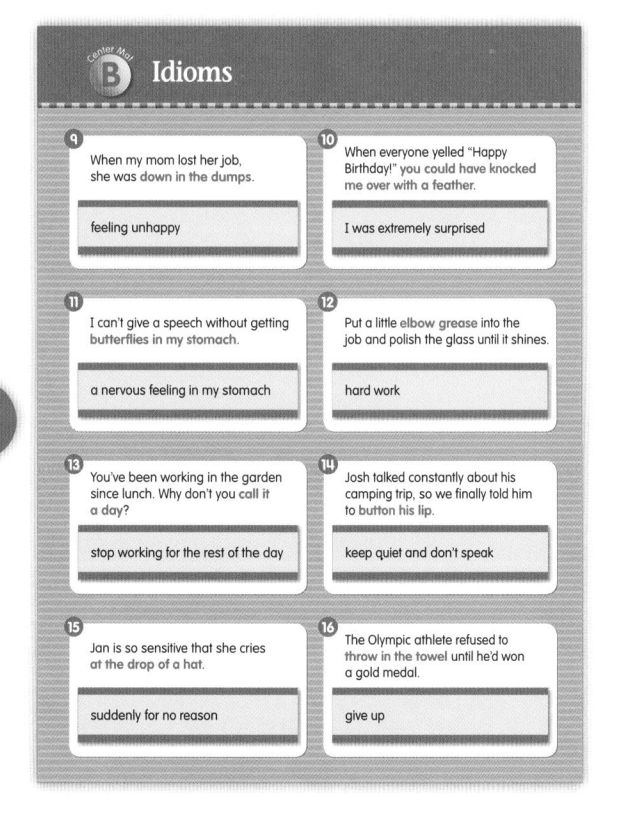

B Idioms

9 When my mom lost her job, she was down in the dumps.

feeling unhappy

10 When everyone yelled "Happy Birthday!" you could have knocked me over with a feather.

I was extremely surprised

11 I can't give a speech without getting butterflies in my stomach.

a nervous feeling in my stomach

12 Put a little elbow grease into the job and polish the glass until it shines.

hard work

13 You've been working in the garden since lunch. Why don't you call it a day?

stop working for the rest of the day

14 Josh talked constantly about his camping trip, so we finally told him to button his lip.

keep quiet and don't speak

15 Jan is so sensitive that she cries at the drop of a hat.

suddenly for no reason

16 The Olympic athlete refused to throw in the towel until he'd won a gold medal.

give up

1

Don't get so upset—you're **making a mountain out of a molehill**.

2

Don't worry, I'll be at the party **with bells on**!

3

I **fly off the handle** whenever anyone calls me "kiddo."

4

In restaurants, my little cousin is like a **bull in a china shop**.

5

Pablo is a **night owl**, so he often sleeps late in the morning.

6

A little birdie told me that you're mad at me. Is it true?

7

I almost missed the bus this morning, but I made it **by the skin of my teeth**.

8

You can argue until you're **blue in the face**, but you'll never convince me.

Take It to Your Seat Centers—Reading & Language • EMC 2845 • © Evan-Moor Corp.

9

When my mom lost her job, she was **down in the dumps**.

10

When everyone yelled "Happy Birthday!" **you could have knocked me over with a feather**.

11

I can't give a speech without getting **butterflies in my stomach**.

12

Put a little **elbow grease** into the job and polish the glass until it shines.

13

You've been working in the garden since lunch. Why don't you **call it a day**?

14

Josh talked constantly about his camping trip, so we finally told him to **button his lip**.

15

Jan is so sensitive that she cries **at the drop of a hat**.

16

The Olympic athlete refused to **throw in the towel** until he'd won a gold medal.

get very angry	I was extremely surprised
I was told by someone whose name I won't mention	in a happy mood and ready to celebrate
person who is extremely clumsy	keep quiet and don't speak
making a big deal out of a minor problem	stop working for the rest of the day
person who likes to stay up late	hard work
feeling unhappy	a nervous feeling in my stomach
suddenly for no reason	give up
exhausted	just barely in time

Idioms

Take It to Your Seat Centers
Reading & Language
EMC 2845 • © Evan-Moor Corp.

Idioms

Take It to Your Seat Centers
Reading & Language
EMC 2845 • © Evan-Moor Corp.

Idioms

Take It to Your Seat Centers
Reading & Language
EMC 2845 • © Evan-Moor Corp.

Idioms

Take It to Your Seat Centers
Reading & Language
EMC 2845 • © Evan-Moor Corp.

Idioms

Take It to Your Seat Centers
Reading & Language
EMC 2845 • © Evan-Moor Corp.

Idioms

Take It to Your Seat Centers
Reading & Language
EMC 2845 • © Evan-Moor Corp.

Idioms

Take It to Your Seat Centers
Reading & Language
EMC 2845 • © Evan-Moor Corp.

Idioms

Take It to Your Seat Centers
Reading & Language
EMC 2845 • © Evan-Moor Corp.

Idioms

Take It to Your Seat Centers
Reading & Language
EMC 2845 • © Evan-Moor Corp.

Idioms

Take It to Your Seat Centers
Reading & Language
EMC 2845 • © Evan-Moor Corp.

Idioms

Take It to Your Seat Centers
Reading & Language
EMC 2845 • © Evan-Moor Corp.

Idioms

Take It to Your Seat Centers
Reading & Language
EMC 2845 • © Evan-Moor Corp.

Idioms

Take It to Your Seat Centers
Reading & Language
EMC 2845 • © Evan-Moor Corp.

Idioms

Take It to Your Seat Centers
Reading & Language
EMC 2845 • © Evan-Moor Corp.

Idioms

Take It to Your Seat Centers
Reading & Language
EMC 2845 • © Evan-Moor Corp.

Idioms

Take It to Your Seat Centers
Reading & Language
EMC 2845 • © Evan-Moor Corp.

Synonyms/Antonyms

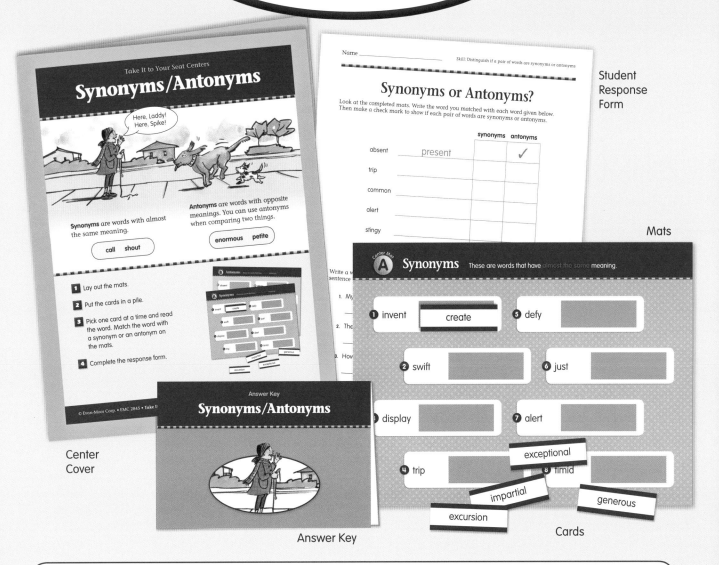

Center Cover

Answer Key

Student Response Form

Mats

Cards

Skill
Distinguish if a pair of words are synonyms
or antonyms

Prepare the Center
Follow the directions on page 3.

Introduce the Center
Demonstrate how to use the center. State the goal:
*You will read each card and place it on the mat below
the correct category.*

Synonyms or Antonyms?

Look at the completed mats. Write the word you matched with each word given below.
Then make a check mark to show if each pair of words are synonyms or antonyms.

		synonyms	antonyms
absent	present		✓
trip			
common			
alert			
stingy			
swift			

Write a word from the center that could replace the boldfaced word in each
sentence below. Is it an antonym or a synonym?

1. My brother always seems to want to **resist** the rules at school.

   _____

2. The captain gave the order to **retreat** as the battle wore on after dark.

   _____

3. How did you know that I **detest** sour cherry candies?

   _____

Synonyms/Antonyms

Synonyms are words with almost the same meaning.

(call   shout)

Antonyms are words with opposite meanings. You can use antonyms when comparing two things.

(enormous   petite)

1 Lay out the mats.

2 Put the cards in a pile.

3 Pick one card at a time and read the word. Match the word with a synonym or an antonym on the mats.

4 Complete the response form.

Synonyms or Antonyms?

Look at the completed mats. Write the word you matched with each word given below.
Then make a check mark to show if each pair of words are synonyms or antonyms.

	synonyms	antonyms
absent	present	✓
trip	excursion	✓
common	exceptional		✓
alert	vigilant	✓
stingy	generous		✓
swift	fleet	✓

Write a word from the center that could replace the boldfaced word in each sentence below. Is it an antonym or a synonym?

1. My brother always seems to want to **resist** the rules at school.

   defy   (synonym)

2. The captain gave the order to **retreat** as the battle wore on after dark.

   advance   (antonym)

3. How did you know that I **detest** sour cherry candies?

   adore   (antonym)

(fold)

Answer Key

Synonyms/Antonyms

Answer Key
Synonyms/Antonyms

A

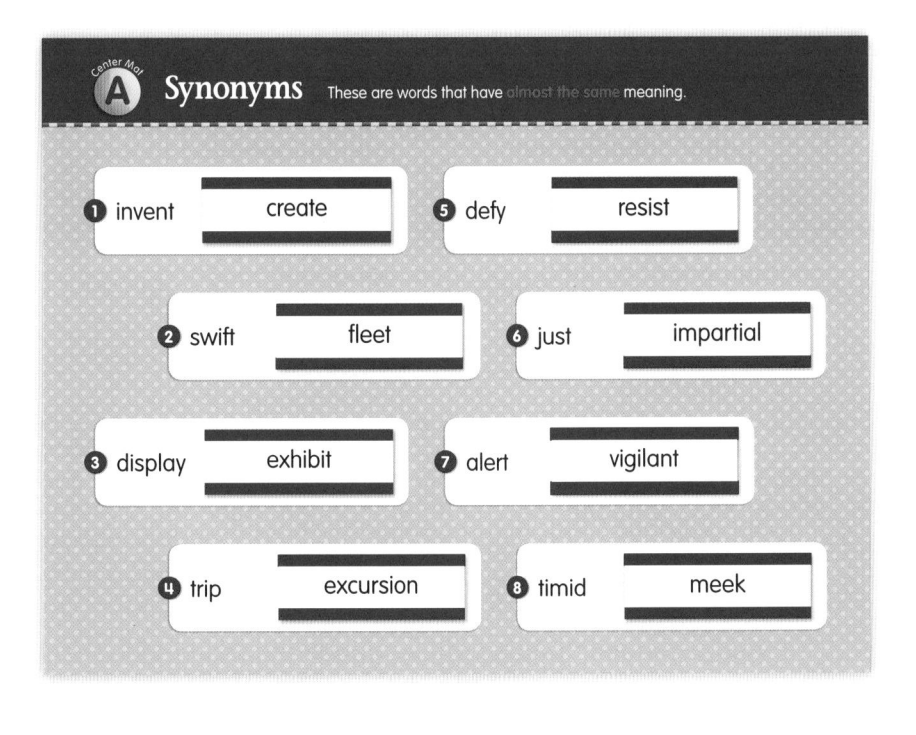

A Synonyms These are words that have almost the same meaning.

1. invent — create
2. swift — fleet
3. display — exhibit
4. trip — excursion
5. defy — resist
6. just — impartial
7. alert — vigilant
8. timid — meek

B

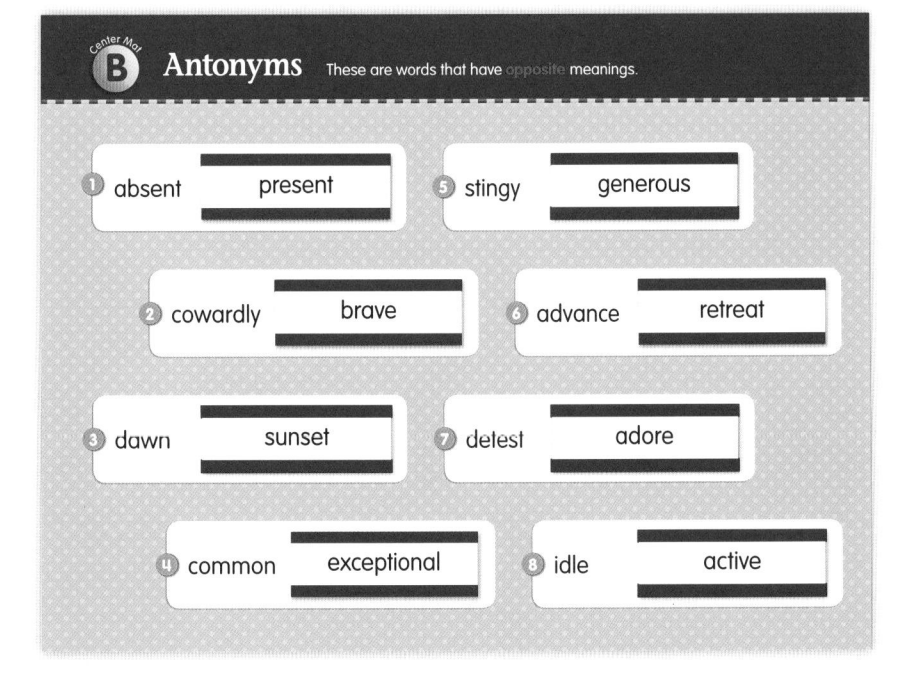

B Antonyms These are words that have opposite meanings.

1. absent — present
2. cowardly — brave
3. dawn — sunset
4. common — exceptional
5. stingy — generous
6. advance — retreat
7. detest — adore
8. idle — active

Synonyms

These are words that have almost the same meaning.

5 defy

6 just

7 alert

8 timid

1 invent

2 swift

3 display

4 trip

Take It to Your Seat Centers—Reading & Language • EMC 2845 • © Evan-Moor Corp.

Antonyms

These are words that have opposite meanings.

1 absent

5 stingy

2 cowardly

6 advance

3 dawn

7 detest

4 common

8 idle

Take It to Your Seat Centers—Reading & Language • EMC 2845 • © Evan-Moor Corp.

Synonyms	Antonyms
create	present
exhibit	exceptional
vigilant	active
fleet	brave
resist	generous
meek	adore
impartial	sunset
excursion	retreat

Synonyms/Antonyms

Take It to Your Seat Centers
Reading & Language
EMC 2845 • © Evan-Moor Corp.

Synonyms/Antonyms

Take It to Your Seat Centers
Reading & Language
EMC 2845 • © Evan-Moor Corp.

Synonyms/Antonyms

Take It to Your Seat Centers
Reading & Language
EMC 2845 • © Evan-Moor Corp.

Synonyms/Antonyms

Take It to Your Seat Centers
Reading & Language
EMC 2845 • © Evan-Moor Corp.

Synonyms/Antonyms

Take It to Your Seat Centers
Reading & Language
EMC 2845 • © Evan-Moor Corp.

Synonyms/Antonyms

Take It to Your Seat Centers
Reading & Language
EMC 2845 • © Evan-Moor Corp.

Synonyms/Antonyms

Take It to Your Seat Centers
Reading & Language
EMC 2845 • © Evan-Moor Corp.

Synonyms/Antonyms

Take It to Your Seat Centers
Reading & Language
EMC 2845 • © Evan-Moor Corp.

Synonyms/Antonyms

Take It to Your Seat Centers
Reading & Language
EMC 2845 • © Evan-Moor Corp.

Synonyms/Antonyms

Take It to Your Seat Centers
Reading & Language
EMC 2845 • © Evan-Moor Corp.

Synonyms/Antonyms

Take It to Your Seat Centers
Reading & Language
EMC 2845 • © Evan-Moor Corp.

Synonyms/Antonyms

Take It to Your Seat Centers
Reading & Language
EMC 2845 • © Evan-Moor Corp.

Synonyms/Antonyms

Take It to Your Seat Centers
Reading & Language
EMC 2845 • © Evan-Moor Corp.

Synonyms/Antonyms

Take It to Your Seat Centers
Reading & Language
EMC 2845 • © Evan-Moor Corp.

Synonyms/Antonyms

Take It to Your Seat Centers
Reading & Language
EMC 2845 • © Evan-Moor Corp.

Synonyms/Antonyms

Take It to Your Seat Centers
Reading & Language
EMC 2845 • © Evan-Moor Corp.

Homophones

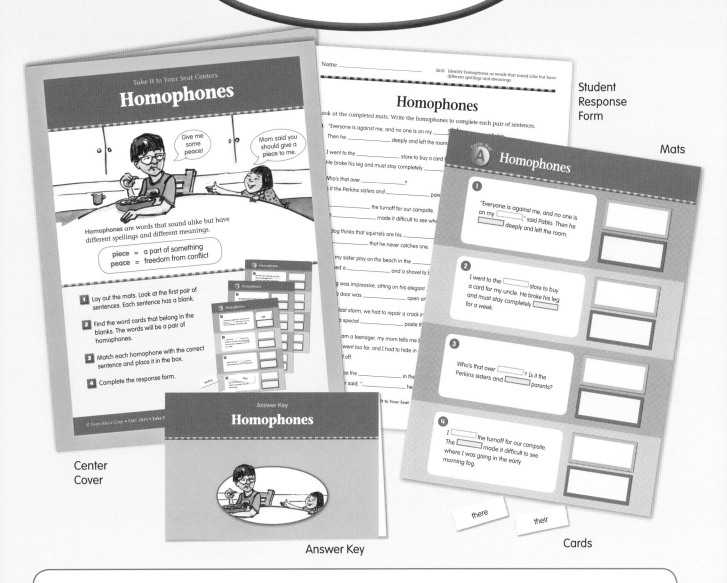

Center Cover

Answer Key

Student Response Form

Mats

Cards

Skill
Identify homophones as words that sound alike but have different spellings and meanings

Prepare the Center
Follow the directions on page 3.

Introduce the Center
Demonstrate how to use the center. State the goal: *You will read pairs of sentences that have missing homophones, then find the word card that completes each sentence and place it in the correct box.*

Homophones

Look at the completed mats. Write the homophones to complete each pair of sentences.

1. "Everyone is against me, and no one is on my ____side____," said Pablo.

   Then he _____ deeply and left the room.

2. I went to the _____ store to buy a card for my uncle.

   He broke his leg and must stay completely _____ for a week.

3. Who's that over _____?

   Is it the Perkins sisters and _____ parents?

4. I _____ the turnoff for our campsite.

   The _____ made it difficult to see where I was going in the early morning fog.

5. My dog thinks that squirrels are his _____.

   I _____ that he never catches one.

6. I saw my sister play on the beach in the _____ morning light.

   She used a _____ and a shovel to build a sand castle.

7. The king was impressive, sitting on his elegant _____.

   Soon the door was _____ open and the queen joined him.

8. After the last storm, we had to repair a crack in our kitchen _____.

   We used a special _____ paste that quickly filled in the crack.

9. Now that I am a teenager, my mom tells me I get bigger and _____ every day.

   Last week I went too far, and I had to hide in the yard behind a _____ until
   Mom cooled off.

10. It is hard to see the _____ in the movie theater when the lights are dimmed.

    The nice usher said, "_____ help you find your seats with this flashlight."

Homophones

Homophones are words that sound alike but have different spellings and different meanings.

> **piece** = a part of something
> **peace** = freedom from conflict

1 Lay out the mats. Look at the first pair of sentences. Each sentence has a blank.

2 Find the word cards that belong in the blanks. The words will be a pair of homophones.

3 Match each homophone with the correct sentence and place it in the box.

4 Complete the response form.

Homophones

Look at the completed mats. Write the homophones to complete each pair of sentences.

1. "Everyone is against me, and no one is on my _____ side _____," said Pablo.
   Then he _____ sighed _____ deeply and left the room.

2. I went to the _____ stationery _____ store to buy a card for my uncle.
   He broke his leg and must stay completely _____ stationary _____ for a week.

3. Who's that over _____ there _____?
   Is it the Perkins sisters and _____ their _____ parents?

4. I _____ missed _____ the turnoff for our campsite.
   The _____ mist _____ made it difficult to see where I was going in the early morning fog.

5. My dog thinks that squirrels are his _____ herd _____.
   I _____ heard _____ that he never catches one.

6. I saw my sister play on the beach in the _____ pale _____ morning light.
   She used a _____ pail _____ and a shovel to build a sand castle.

7. The king was impressive, sitting on his elegant _____ throne _____.
   Soon the door was _____ thrown _____ open and the queen joined him.

8. After the last storm, we had to repair a crack in our kitchen _____ ceiling _____.
   We used a special _____ sealing _____ paste that quickly filled in the crack.

9. Now that I am a teenager, my mom tells me I get bigger and _____ bolder _____ every day.
   Last week I went too far, and I had to hide in the yard behind a _____ boulder _____ until Mom cooled off.

10. It is hard to see the _____ aisle _____ in the movie theater when the lights are dimmed.
    The nice usher said, "_____ I'll _____ help you find your seats with this flashlight."

Response Form

(fold)

Answer Key

Homophones

Answer Key

Homophones

A — Homophones

1. "Everyone is against me, and no one is on my **side**," said Pablo. Then he **sighed** deeply and left the room. [side / sighed]

2. I went to the **stationery** store to buy a card for my uncle. He broke his leg and must stay completely **stationary** for a week. [stationery / stationary]

3. Who's that **there** over **there**? Is it the Perkins sisters and **their** parents? [there / their]

4. I **missed** the turnoff for our campsite. The **mist** made it difficult to see where I was going in the early morning fog. [missed / mist]

B — Homophones

5. My dog thinks that squirrels are his **prey**. I **pray** that he never catches one. [prey / pray]

6. I saw my sister play on the beach in the **pale** morning light. She used a **pail** and a shovel to build a sand castle. [pale / pail]

7. The king was impressive, sitting on his elegant **throne**. Soon the door was **thrown** open and the queen joined him. [throne / thrown]

8. After the last storm, we had to repair a crack in our kitchen **ceiling**. We used a special **sealing** paste that quickly filled in the crack. [ceiling / sealing]

C — Homophones

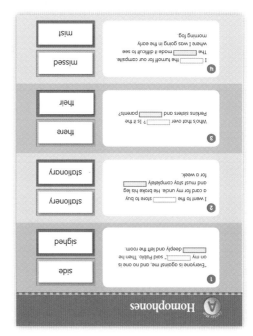

9. Now that I am a teenager, my mom tells me I get bigger and **bolder** every day. Last week I went too far, and I had to hide in the yard behind a **boulder** until Mom cooled off. [bolder / boulder]

10. It is hard to see the **aisle** in the movie theater when the lights are dimmed. The nice usher said, "**I'll** help you find your seats with this flashlight." [aisle / I'll]

11. I can't stop eating this delicious corn that is **grown** in our garden. I **groan** as I leave the table because I am so very full. [grown / groan]

12. The cowboys guided the **herd** of cattle across the desert. I **heard** the stomping of hooves as they galloped along. [herd / heard]

1

"Everyone is against me, and no one is on my ⬚⬚⬚," said Pablo. Then he ⬚⬚⬚ deeply and left the room.

2

I went to the ⬚⬚⬚ store to buy a card for my uncle. He broke his leg and must stay completely ⬚⬚⬚ for a week.

3

Who's that over ⬚⬚⬚? Is it the Perkins sisters and ⬚⬚⬚ parents?

4

I ⬚⬚⬚ the turnoff for our campsite. The ⬚⬚⬚ made it difficult to see where I was going in the early morning fog.

B Homophones

5

My dog thinks that squirrels are his ☐. I ☐ that he never catches one.

6

I saw my sister play on the beach in the ☐ morning light. She used a ☐ and a shovel to build a sand castle.

7

The king was impressive, sitting on his elegant ☐. Soon the door was ☐ open and the queen joined him.

8

After the last storm, we had to repair a crack in our kitchen ☐. We used a special ☐ paste that quickly filled in the crack.

9

Now that I am a teenager, my mom tells me I get bigger and [ ] every day. Last week I went too far, and I had to hide in the yard behind a [ ] until Mom cooled off.

10

It is hard to see the [ ] in the movie theater when the lights are dimmed. The nice usher said, " [ ] help you find your seats with this flashlight."

11

I can't stop eating this delicious corn that is [ ] in our garden. I [ ] as I leave the table because I am so very full.

12

The cowboys guided the [ ] of cattle across the desert. I [ ] the stomping of hooves as they galloped along.

I'll	ceiling	grown
herd	throne	boulder
groan	aisle	sealing
bolder	heard	thrown
there	stationary	pail
prey	missed	sighed
pale	their	stationery
side	pray	mist

Homophones Take It to Your Seat Centers Reading & Language EMC 2845 • © Evan-Moor Corp.	**Homophones** Take It to Your Seat Centers Reading & Language EMC 2845 • © Evan-Moor Corp.	**Homophones** Take It to Your Seat Centers Reading & Language EMC 2845 • © Evan-Moor Corp.
Homophones Take It to Your Seat Centers Reading & Language EMC 2845 • © Evan-Moor Corp.	**Homophones** Take It to Your Seat Centers Reading & Language EMC 2845 • © Evan-Moor Corp.	**Homophones** Take It to Your Seat Centers Reading & Language EMC 2845 • © Evan-Moor Corp.
Homophones Take It to Your Seat Centers Reading & Language EMC 2845 • © Evan-Moor Corp.	**Homophones** Take It to Your Seat Centers Reading & Language EMC 2845 • © Evan-Moor Corp.	**Homophones** Take It to Your Seat Centers Reading & Language EMC 2845 • © Evan-Moor Corp.
Homophones Take It to Your Seat Centers Reading & Language EMC 2845 • © Evan-Moor Corp.	**Homophones** Take It to Your Seat Centers Reading & Language EMC 2845 • © Evan-Moor Corp.	**Homophones** Take It to Your Seat Centers Reading & Language EMC 2845 • © Evan-Moor Corp.
Homophones Take It to Your Seat Centers Reading & Language EMC 2845 • © Evan-Moor Corp.	**Homophones** Take It to Your Seat Centers Reading & Language EMC 2845 • © Evan-Moor Corp.	**Homophones** Take It to Your Seat Centers Reading & Language EMC 2845 • © Evan-Moor Corp.
Homophones Take It to Your Seat Centers Reading & Language EMC 2845 • © Evan-Moor Corp.	**Homophones** Take It to Your Seat Centers Reading & Language EMC 2845 • © Evan-Moor Corp.	**Homophones** Take It to Your Seat Centers Reading & Language EMC 2845 • © Evan-Moor Corp.
Homophones Take It to Your Seat Centers Reading & Language EMC 2845 • © Evan-Moor Corp.	**Homophones** Take It to Your Seat Centers Reading & Language EMC 2845 • © Evan-Moor Corp.	**Homophones** Take It to Your Seat Centers Reading & Language EMC 2845 • © Evan-Moor Corp.
Homophones Take It to Your Seat Centers Reading & Language EMC 2845 • © Evan-Moor Corp.	**Homophones** Take It to Your Seat Centers Reading & Language EMC 2845 • © Evan-Moor Corp.	**Homophones** Take It to Your Seat Centers Reading & Language EMC 2845 • © Evan-Moor Corp.

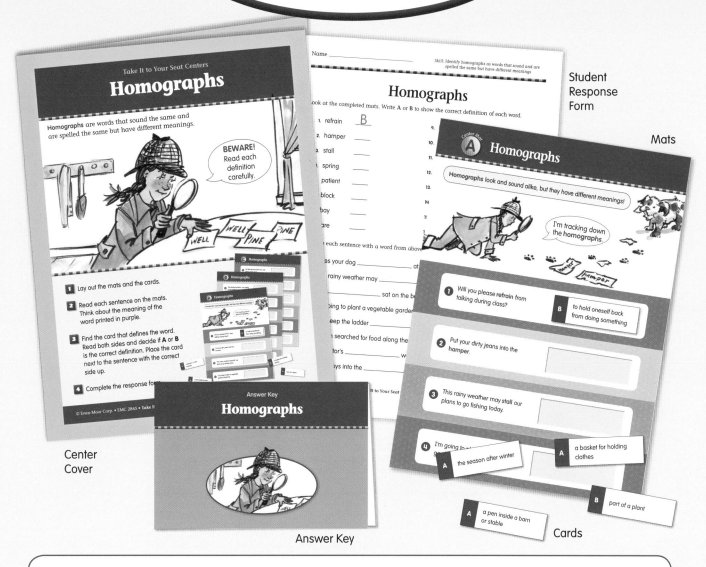

Student Response Form

Center Cover

Answer Key

Mats

Cards

Skill
Identify homographs as words that sound and are spelled the same but have different meanings

Prepare the Center
Follow the directions on page 3.

Introduce the Center
Demonstrate how to use the center. State the goal: *You will read each sentence containing a homograph, then place a definition card on the mat to show the meaning of the homograph.*

Homographs

Look at the completed mats. Write **A** or **B** to show the correct definition of each word.

1. refrain __B__

2. hamper _____

3. stall _____

4. spring _____

5. patient _____

6. block _____

7. bay _____

8. rare _____

9. land _____

10. pitcher _____

11. trunk _____

12. leaves _____

13. watch _____

14. stable _____

15. bed _____

16. graze _____

Complete each sentence with a word from above.

1. Does your dog _____ at the full moon?

2. This rainy weather may _____ our plans to go fishing today.

3. The _____ sat on the bench during the whole game.

4. I'm going to plant a vegetable garden this _____.

5. I will keep the ladder _____ as you climb up to the roof.

6. The fish searched for food along the creek _____.

7. The doctor's _____ was sitting in the waiting room.

8. Put the toys into the _____ and clean up the room.

Homographs

Homographs are words that sound the same and are spelled the same but have different meanings.

BEWARE! Read each definition carefully.

I'm tracking down the homographs

1 Lay out the mats and the cards.

2 Read each sentence on the mats. Think about the meaning of the word printed in purple.

3 Find the card that defines the word. Read both sides and decide if **A** or **B** is the correct definition. Place the card next to the sentence with the correct side up.

4 Complete the response form.

Homographs

Answer Key

Response Form

Homographs

Look at the completed mats. Write **A** or **B** to show the correct definition of each word.

1.	refrain	B	9.	land	B
2.	hamper	A	10.	pitcher	B
3.	stall	B	11.	trunk	A
4.	spring	A	12.	leaves	A
5.	patient	B	13.	watch	B
6.	block	B	14.	stable	B
7.	bay	B	15.	bed	A
8.	rare	A	16.	graze	A

Complete each sentence with a word from above.

1. Does your dog ___bay___ at the full moon?
2. This rainy weather may ___stall___ our plans to go fishing today.
3. The ___pitcher___ sat on the bench during the whole game.
4. I'm going to plant a vegetable garden this ___spring___.
5. I will keep the ladder ___stable___ as you climb up to the roof.
6. The fish searched for food along the creek ___bed___.
7. The doctor's ___patient___ was sitting in the waiting room.
8. Put the toys into the ___trunk___ and clean up the room.

Homographs A

Homographs look and sound alike, but they have different meanings!

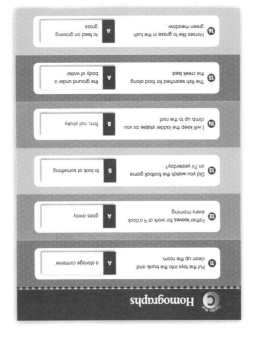

I'm tracking down the homographs.

1. Will you please refrain from talking during class? — **B** to hold oneself back from doing something
2. Put your dirty jeans into the hamper. — **A** a basket for holding clothes
3. This rainy weather may stall our plans to go fishing today. — **B** to delay
4. I'm going to plant a vegetable garden this spring. — **A** the season after winter

Homographs B

5. The doctor's patient was sitting in the waiting room. — **B** a person being treated by a doctor
6. Mario rode his new bike around the block. — **A** an area in a city enclosed by four streets
7. Does your dog bay at the full moon? — **A** to let out a long, howling bark
8. It is rare for me to have a soft drink. — **A** unusual, not often
9. Did you see that butterfly land on the sunflower? — **B** to come to rest
10. The pitcher sat on the bench during the whole game. — **B** a member of a ball team

Homographs C

11. Put the toys into the trunk and clean up the room. — **A** a storage container
12. Father leaves for work at 9 o'clock every morning. — **A** goes away
13. Did you watch the football game on TV yesterday? — **B** to look at something
14. I will keep the ladder stable as you climb up to the roof. — **B** firm, not shaky
15. The fish searched for food along the ground under a body of water. — **A** the creek bed
16. Horses like to graze in the lush green meadow. — **A** to feed on growing grass

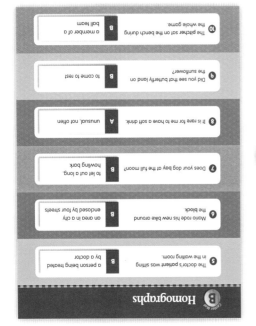

Homographs look and sound alike, but they have different meanings!

I'm tracking down the **homographs**.

1. Will you please **refrain** from talking during class?

2. Put your dirty jeans into the **hamper**.

3. This rainy weather may **stall** our plans to go fishing today.

4. I'm going to plant a vegetable garden this **spring**.

5 The doctor's **patient** was sitting in the waiting room.

6 Mario rode his new bike around the **block**.

7 Does your dog **bay** at the full moon?

8 It is **rare** for me to have a soft drink.

9 Did you see that butterfly **land** on the sunflower?

10 The **pitcher** sat on the bench during the whole game.

Take It to Your Seat Centers—Reading & Language • EMC 2845 • © Evan-Moor Corp.

11 Put the toys into the **trunk** and clean up the room.

12 Father **leaves** for work at 9 o'clock every morning.

13 Did you **watch** the football game on TV yesterday?

14 I will keep the ladder **stable** as you climb up to the roof.

15 The fish searched for food along the creek **bed**.

16 Horses like to **graze** in the lush green meadow.

Take It to Your Seat Centers—Reading & Language • EMC 2845 • © Evan-Moor Corp.

A	a basket for holding clothes	**A**	a container for a liquid
A	a pen inside a barn or stable	**A**	a storage container
A	the season after winter	**A**	goes away
A	waiting in a calm manner	**A**	something used to tell time
A	to keep something from passing through	**A**	a building where animals are kept
A	where the ocean cuts into the coastline	**A**	the ground under a body of water
A	unusual, not often	**A**	to feed on growing grass
A	a part of Earth's crust	**A**	the chorus of a song

B	a member of a ball team	**B**	to keep from moving or acting freely
B	an elephant's nose	**B**	to delay
B	part of a plant	**B**	a small stream of water coming from the ground
B	to look at something	**B**	a person being treated by a doctor
B	firm, not shaky	**B**	an area in a city enclosed by four streets
B	something to sleep on	**B**	to let out a long, howling bark
B	to scrape	**B**	cooked for only a short time
B	to hold oneself back from doing something	**B**	to come to rest

Prefixes

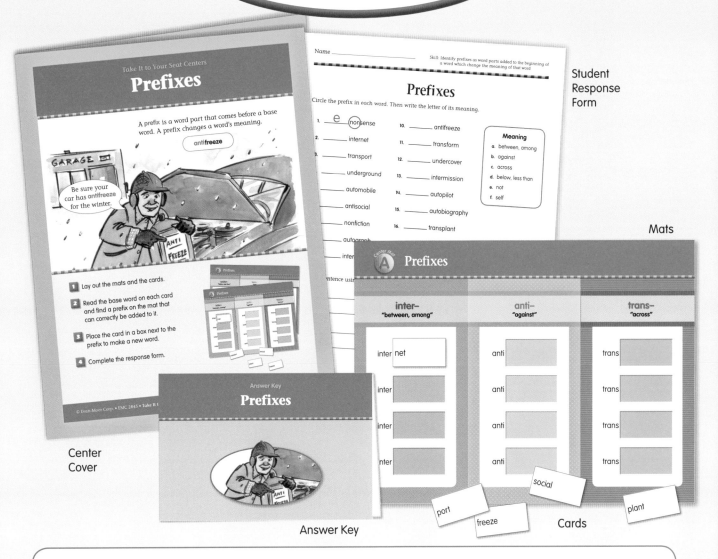

Student
Response
Form

Mats

Center
Cover

Answer Key

Cards

Skill
Identify prefixes as word parts added to the beginning of a word which change the meaning of that word

Prepare the Center
Follow the directions on page 3.

Introduce the Center
Demonstrate how to use the center. State the goal: *You will read each word card and place it on the mat under a prefix that can be added to that word to make a new word.*

Prefixes

Circle the prefix in each word. Then write the letter of its meaning.

1. ___e___ (non)sense

2. _____ internet

3. _____ transport

4. _____ underground

5. _____ automobile

6. _____ antisocial

7. _____ nonfiction

8. _____ autograph

9. _____ international

10. _____ antifreeze

11. _____ transform

12. _____ undercover

13. _____ intermission

14. _____ autopilot

15. _____ autobiography

16. _____ transplant

17. _____ underpaid

18. _____ antislavery

Meaning

a. between, among

b. against

c. across

d. below, less than

e. not

f. self

Write a sentence using each word below.

sense _____

_____

nonsense _____

_____

Prefixes

A **prefix** is a word part that comes before a base word. A prefix changes a word's meaning.

anti**freeze**

Be sure your car has **antifreeze** for the winter.

1 Lay out the mats and the cards.

2 Read the base word on each card and find a prefix on the mat that can correctly be added to it.

3 Place the card in a box next to the prefix to make a new word.

4 Complete the response form.

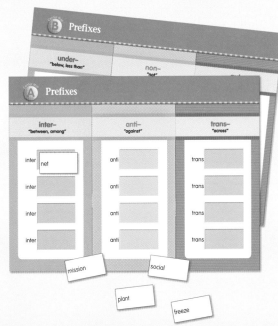

Response Form

Prefixes

Circle the prefix in each word. Then write the letter of its meaning.

Meaning
a. between, among
b. against
c. across
d. below, less than
e. not
f. self

1. e nonsense
2. a internet
3. c transport
4. d underground
5. f automobile
6. b antisocial
7. e nonfiction
8. f autograph
9. a international

10. b antifreeze
11. c transform
12. d undercover
13. a intermission
14. f autopilot
15. f autobiography
16. c transplant
17. d underpaid
18. b antislavery

Write a sentence using each word below.
Answers will vary.

sense
_____
_____
nonsense
_____
_____

(fold)

Answer Key

Prefixes

Prefixes

A Prefixes

inter– "between, among"	anti– "against"	trans– "across"
inter net	anti septic	trans form
inter national	anti slavery	trans port
inter mission	anti social	trans plant
inter twine	anti freeze	trans pose

B Prefixes

under– "below, less than"	non– "not"	auto– "self"
under ground	non fiction	auto graph
under cover	non sense	auto biography
under paid	non stop	auto mobile
under fed	non violent	auto pilot

Center Mat

Prefixes

trans–
"across"

| trans | trans | trans | trans |

anti–
"against"

| anti | anti | anti | anti |

inter–
"between, among"

| inter | inter | inter | inter |

Prefixes

Center Mat **B**

auto–
"self"

| auto | auto | auto | auto |

non–
"not"

| non | non | non | non |

under–
"below, less than"

| under | under | under | under |

net	form	fiction
national	port	sense
mission	plant	stop
septic	ground	graph
slavery	cover	biography
social	paid	mobile
violent	twine	freeze
pilot	pose	fed

Prefixes Take It to Your Seat Centers Reading & Language EMC 2845 • © Evan-Moor Corp.	**Prefixes** Take It to Your Seat Centers Reading & Language EMC 2845 • © Evan-Moor Corp.	**Prefixes** Take It to Your Seat Centers Reading & Language EMC 2845 • © Evan-Moor Corp.
Prefixes Take It to Your Seat Centers Reading & Language EMC 2845 • © Evan-Moor Corp.	**Prefixes** Take It to Your Seat Centers Reading & Language EMC 2845 • © Evan-Moor Corp.	**Prefixes** Take It to Your Seat Centers Reading & Language EMC 2845 • © Evan-Moor Corp.
Prefixes Take It to Your Seat Centers Reading & Language EMC 2845 • © Evan-Moor Corp.	**Prefixes** Take It to Your Seat Centers Reading & Language EMC 2845 • © Evan-Moor Corp.	**Prefixes** Take It to Your Seat Centers Reading & Language EMC 2845 • © Evan-Moor Corp.
Prefixes Take It to Your Seat Centers Reading & Language EMC 2845 • © Evan-Moor Corp.	**Prefixes** Take It to Your Seat Centers Reading & Language EMC 2845 • © Evan-Moor Corp.	**Prefixes** Take It to Your Seat Centers Reading & Language EMC 2845 • © Evan-Moor Corp.
Prefixes Take It to Your Seat Centers Reading & Language EMC 2845 • © Evan-Moor Corp.	**Prefixes** Take It to Your Seat Centers Reading & Language EMC 2845 • © Evan-Moor Corp.	**Prefixes** Take It to Your Seat Centers Reading & Language EMC 2845 • © Evan-Moor Corp.
Prefixes Take It to Your Seat Centers Reading & Language EMC 2845 • © Evan-Moor Corp.	**Prefixes** Take It to Your Seat Centers Reading & Language EMC 2845 • © Evan-Moor Corp.	**Prefixes** Take It to Your Seat Centers Reading & Language EMC 2845 • © Evan-Moor Corp.
Prefixes Take It to Your Seat Centers Reading & Language EMC 2845 • © Evan-Moor Corp.	**Prefixes** Take It to Your Seat Centers Reading & Language EMC 2845 • © Evan-Moor Corp.	**Prefixes** Take It to Your Seat Centers Reading & Language EMC 2845 • © Evan-Moor Corp.
Prefixes Take It to Your Seat Centers Reading & Language EMC 2845 • © Evan-Moor Corp.	**Prefixes** Take It to Your Seat Centers Reading & Language EMC 2845 • © Evan-Moor Corp.	**Prefixes** Take It to Your Seat Centers Reading & Language EMC 2845 • © Evan-Moor Corp.

Suffixes

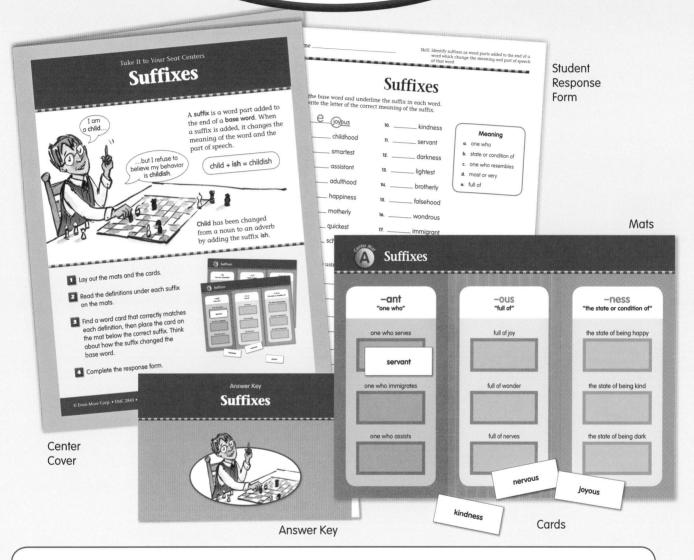

Center Cover

Student Response Form

Mats

Answer Key

Cards

Skill

Identify suffixes as word parts added to the end of a word which change the meaning and part of speech of that word

Prepare the Center

Follow the directions on page 3.

Introduce the Center

Demonstrate how to use the center. State the goal: *You will read a word card, then find its suffix on a mat and place the card under the correct definition.*

Name _____

Skill: Identify suffixes as word parts added to the end of a word which change the meaning and part of speech of that word

Suffixes

Circle the base word and underline the suffix in each word.
Then write the letter of the correct meaning of the suffix.

1. __e__ (joy)ous

2. _____ childhood

3. _____ smartest

4. _____ assistant

5. _____ adulthood

6. _____ happiness

7. _____ motherly

8. _____ quickest

9. _____ scholarly

10. _____ kindness

11. _____ servant

12. _____ darkness

13. _____ lightest

14. _____ brotherly

15. _____ falsehood

16. _____ wondrous

17. _____ immigrant

18. _____ nervous

Meaning

a. one who

b. state or condition of

c. one who resembles

d. most or very

e. full of

Write a sentence using each word below.

1. serve _____

   servant _____

2. quick _____

   quickest _____

3. kind _____

   kindness _____

Take It to Your Seat Centers—Reading & Language • EMC 2845 • © Evan-Moor Corp.

Suffixes

A **suffix** is a word part added to the end of a **base word**. When a suffix is added, it changes the meaning of the word and the part of speech.

> child + **ish** = childish

Child has been changed from a noun to an adverb by adding the suffix **ish**.

1. Lay out the mats and the cards.

2. Read the definitions under each suffix on the mats.

3. Find a word card that correctly matches each definition, then place the card on the mat below the correct suffix. Think about how the suffix changed the base word.

4. Complete the response form.

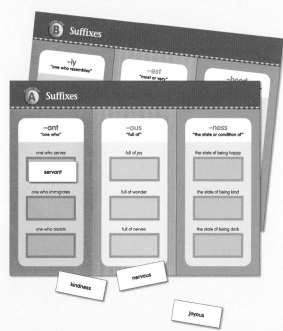

Response Form

Suffixes

Circle the base word and underline the suffix in each word.
Then write the letter of the correct meaning of the suffix.

1.	b	joyous	10.	b	kindness
2.	b	childhood	11.	a	servant
3.	d	smartest	12.	b	darkness
4.	a	assistant	13.	d	lightest
5.	b	adulthood	14.	c	brotherly
6.	b	happiness	15.	b	falsehood
7.	c	motherly	16.	e	wondrous
8.	d	quickest	17.	a	immigrant
9.	c	scholarly	18.	e	nervous

Meaning

- a. one who
- b. state or condition of
- c. one who resembles
- d. most or very
- e. full of

Write a sentence using each word below.

Answers will vary.

1. serve _____
   servant _____
2. quick _____
   quickest _____
3. kind _____
   kindness _____

(fold)

Answer Key

Suffixes

Suffixes

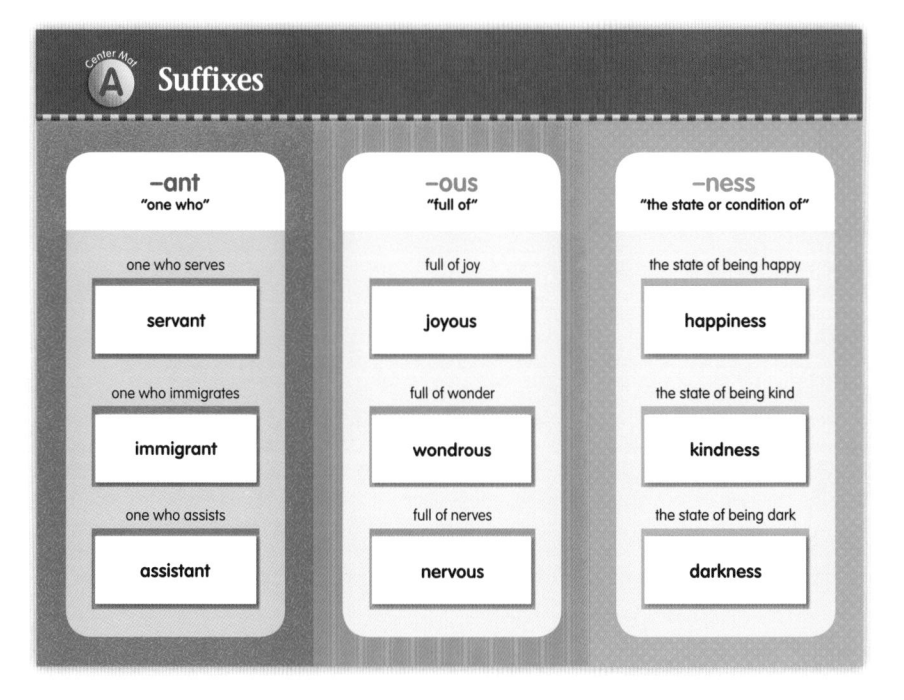

Center Mat

A — Suffixes

–ant
"one who"

one who serves

servant

one who immigrates

immigrant

one who assists

assistant

–ous
"full of"

full of joy

joyous

full of wonder

wondrous

full of nerves

nervous

–ness
"the state or condition of"

the state of being happy

happiness

the state of being kind

kindness

the state of being dark

darkness

Center Mat

B — Suffixes

–ly
"one who resembles"

resembling a mother

motherly

resembling a brother

brotherly

resembling a scholar

scholarly

–est
"most or very"

one who is very smart

smartest

one who is very light

lightest

one who is very quick

quickest

–hood
"the state or condition of"

the state of being a child

childhood

the state of being false

falsehood

the state of being an adult

adulthood

Center Mat

Suffixes

–ant
"one who"

one who serves

one who immigrates

one who assists

–ous
"full of"

full of joy

full of wonder

full of nerves

–ness
"the state or condition of"

the state of being happy

the state of being kind

the state of being dark

Suffixes

-ly
"one who resembles"

resembling a mother

resembling a brother

resembling a scholar

-est
"most or very"

one who is very smart

one who is very light

one who is very quick

-hood
"the state or condition of"

the state of being a child

the state of being false

the state of being an adult

servant	assistant	immigrant
happiness	kindness	darkness
childhood	falsehood	adulthood
smartest	lightest	quickest
motherly	brotherly	scholarly
nervous	joyous	wondrous

Suffixes

Take It to Your Seat Centers
Reading & Language
EMC 2845 • © Evan-Moor Corp.

Suffixes

Take It to Your Seat Centers
Reading & Language
EMC 2845 • © Evan-Moor Corp.

Suffixes

Take It to Your Seat Centers
Reading & Language
EMC 2845 • © Evan-Moor Corp.

Suffixes

Take It to Your Seat Centers
Reading & Language
EMC 2845 • © Evan-Moor Corp.

Suffixes

Take It to Your Seat Centers
Reading & Language
EMC 2845 • © Evan-Moor Corp.

Suffixes

Take It to Your Seat Centers
Reading & Language
EMC 2845 • © Evan-Moor Corp.

Suffixes

Take It to Your Seat Centers
Reading & Language
EMC 2845 • © Evan-Moor Corp.

Suffixes

Take It to Your Seat Centers
Reading & Language
EMC 2845 • © Evan-Moor Corp.

Suffixes

Take It to Your Seat Centers
Reading & Language
EMC 2845 • © Evan-Moor Corp.

Suffixes

Take It to Your Seat Centers
Reading & Language
EMC 2845 • © Evan-Moor Corp.

Suffixes

Take It to Your Seat Centers
Reading & Language
EMC 2845 • © Evan-Moor Corp.

Suffixes

Take It to Your Seat Centers
Reading & Language
EMC 2845 • © Evan-Moor Corp.

Suffixes

Take It to Your Seat Centers
Reading & Language
EMC 2845 • © Evan-Moor Corp.

Suffixes

Take It to Your Seat Centers
Reading & Language
EMC 2845 • © Evan-Moor Corp.

Suffixes

Take It to Your Seat Centers
Reading & Language
EMC 2845 • © Evan-Moor Corp.

Suffixes

Take It to Your Seat Centers
Reading & Language
EMC 2845 • © Evan-Moor Corp.

Suffixes

Take It to Your Seat Centers
Reading & Language
EMC 2845 • © Evan-Moor Corp.

Suffixes

Take It to Your Seat Centers
Reading & Language
EMC 2845 • © Evan-Moor Corp.

Greek and Latin Roots

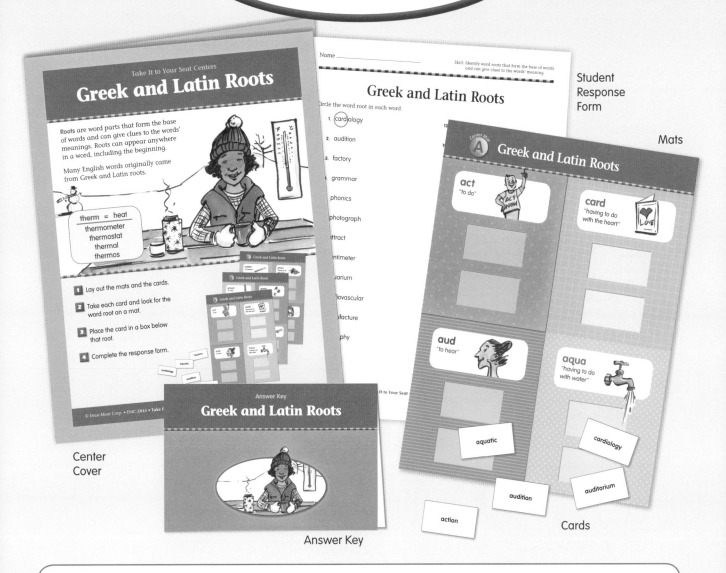

Center Cover

Answer Key

Student Response Form

Mats

Cards

Skill
Identify word roots that form the base of words and can give clues to the words' meanings

Prepare the Center
Follow the directions on page 3.

Introduce the Center
Demonstrate how to use the center. State the goal: *You will read each word card, look for its root, then place the card under the root on the mat that helps give the word its meaning.*

Greek and Latin Roots

Circle the word root in each word.

1. (card)ology

2. audition

3. factory

4. grammar

5. phonics

6. photograph

7. attract

8. centimeter

9. aquarium

10. cardiovascular

11. manufacture

12. biography

13. symphony

14. instruct

15. tractor

16. action

17. auditorium

18. aquatic

19. diagram

20. autograph

21. telephoto

22. destruction

23. thermometer

24. actor

Greek and Latin Roots

Roots are word parts that form the base of words and can give clues to the words' meanings. Roots can appear anywhere in a word, including the beginning.

Many English words originally came from Greek and Latin roots.

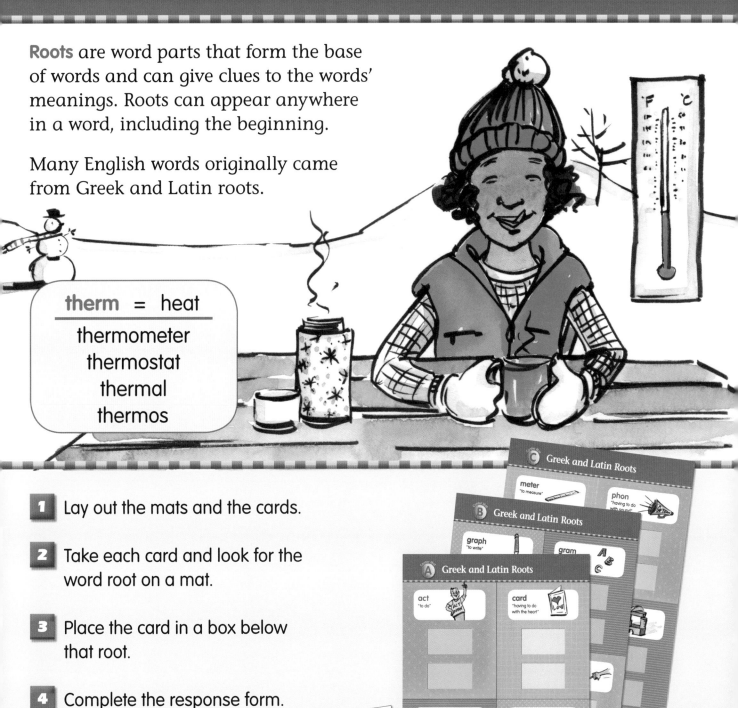

therm = heat
_____
thermometer
thermostat
thermal
thermos

1 Lay out the mats and the cards.

2 Take each card and look for the word root on a mat.

3 Place the card in a box below that root.

4 Complete the response form.

Greek and Latin Roots

Circle the word root in each word.

1. (card)ology	13. (sym)phony
2. (aud)ition	14. in(struct)
3. (fact)ory	15. (tract)or
4. (gram)mar	16. (act)ion
5. (phon)ics	17. (aud)itorium
6. (photo)graph	18. (aqua)tic
7. a(tract)	19. dia(gram)
8. cent(meter)	20. auto(graph)
9. (aqua)rium	21. tele(photo)
10. cardio(vascular)	22. de(struction)
11. manu(facture)	23. thermo(meter)
12. bio(graph)y	24. (act)or

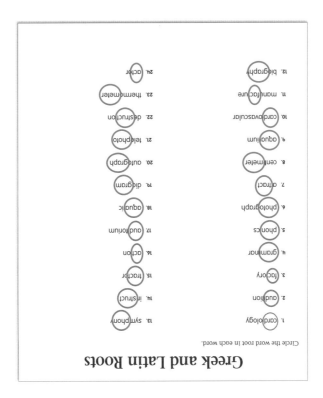

Response Form

(fold)

Answer Key

Greek and Latin Roots

Greek and Latin Roots

Greek and Latin Roots — A

act "to do"

- action
- actor

card "having to do with the heart"

- cardiology
- cardiovascular

aud "to hear"

- auditorium
- audition

aqua "having to do with water"

- aquarium
- aquatic

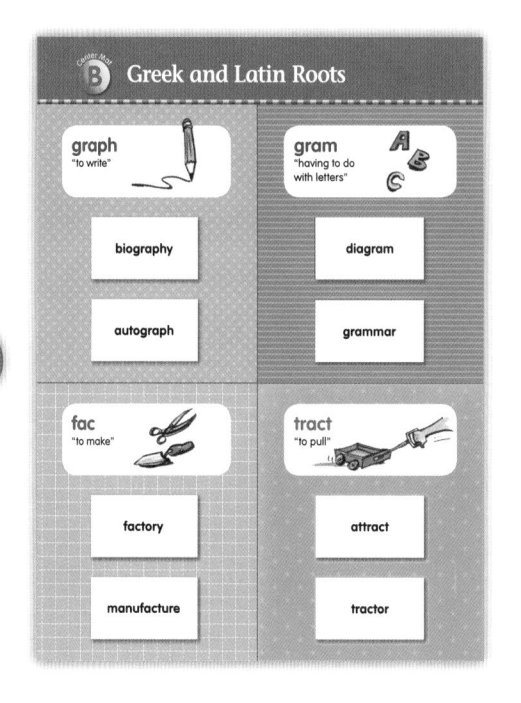

Greek and Latin Roots — B

graph "to write"

- biography
- autograph

gram "having to do with letters"

- diagram
- grammar

fac "to make"

- factory
- manufacture

tract "to pull"

- attract
- tractor

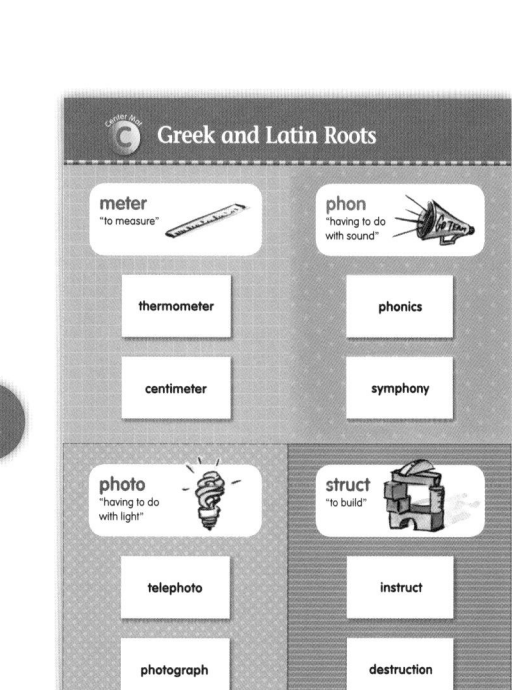

Greek and Latin Roots — C

meter "to measure"

- thermometer
- centimeter

phon "having to do with sound"

- phonics
- symphony

photo "having to do with light"

- telephoto
- photograph

struct "to build"

- instruct
- destruction

Greek and Latin Roots

act
"to do"

card
"having to do with the heart"

aud
"to hear"

aqua
"having to do with water"

Greek and Latin Roots

graph
"to write"

gram
"having to do with letters"

fac
"to make"

tract
"to pull"

Greek and Latin Roots

meter
"to measure"

phon
"having to do with sound"

photo
"having to do with light"

struct
"to build"

cardiology	cardiovascular	auditorium
audition	aquarium	aquatic
factory	manufacture	diagram
grammar	biography	autograph
phonics	symphony	telephoto
photograph	instruct	destruction
attract	tractor	thermometer
centimeter	action	actor

Greek and Latin Roots	Greek and Latin Roots	Greek and Latin Roots
Take It to Your Seat Centers Reading & Language EMC 2845 • © Evan-Moor Corp.	Take It to Your Seat Centers Reading & Language EMC 2845 • © Evan-Moor Corp.	Take It to Your Seat Centers Reading & Language EMC 2845 • © Evan-Moor Corp.
Greek and Latin Roots	Greek and Latin Roots	Greek and Latin Roots
Take It to Your Seat Centers Reading & Language EMC 2845 • © Evan-Moor Corp.	Take It to Your Seat Centers Reading & Language EMC 2845 • © Evan-Moor Corp.	Take It to Your Seat Centers Reading & Language EMC 2845 • © Evan-Moor Corp.
Greek and Latin Roots	Greek and Latin Roots	Greek and Latin Roots
Take It to Your Seat Centers Reading & Language EMC 2845 • © Evan-Moor Corp.	Take It to Your Seat Centers Reading & Language EMC 2845 • © Evan-Moor Corp.	Take It to Your Seat Centers Reading & Language EMC 2845 • © Evan-Moor Corp.
Greek and Latin Roots	Greek and Latin Roots	Greek and Latin Roots
Take It to Your Seat Centers Reading & Language EMC 2845 • © Evan-Moor Corp.	Take It to Your Seat Centers Reading & Language EMC 2845 • © Evan-Moor Corp.	Take It to Your Seat Centers Reading & Language EMC 2845 • © Evan-Moor Corp.
Greek and Latin Roots	Greek and Latin Roots	Greek and Latin Roots
Take It to Your Seat Centers Reading & Language EMC 2845 • © Evan-Moor Corp.	Take It to Your Seat Centers Reading & Language EMC 2845 • © Evan-Moor Corp.	Take It to Your Seat Centers Reading & Language EMC 2845 • © Evan-Moor Corp.
Greek and Latin Roots	Greek and Latin Roots	Greek and Latin Roots
Take It to Your Seat Centers Reading & Language EMC 2845 • © Evan-Moor Corp.	Take It to Your Seat Centers Reading & Language EMC 2845 • © Evan-Moor Corp.	Take It to Your Seat Centers Reading & Language EMC 2845 • © Evan-Moor Corp.
Greek and Latin Roots	Greek and Latin Roots	Greek and Latin Roots
Take It to Your Seat Centers Reading & Language EMC 2845 • © Evan-Moor Corp.	Take It to Your Seat Centers Reading & Language EMC 2845 • © Evan-Moor Corp.	Take It to Your Seat Centers Reading & Language EMC 2845 • © Evan-Moor Corp.
Greek and Latin Roots	Greek and Latin Roots	Greek and Latin Roots
Take It to Your Seat Centers Reading & Language EMC 2845 • © Evan-Moor Corp.	Take It to Your Seat Centers Reading & Language EMC 2845 • © Evan-Moor Corp.	Take It to Your Seat Centers Reading & Language EMC 2845 • © Evan-Moor Corp.

Parts of Speech

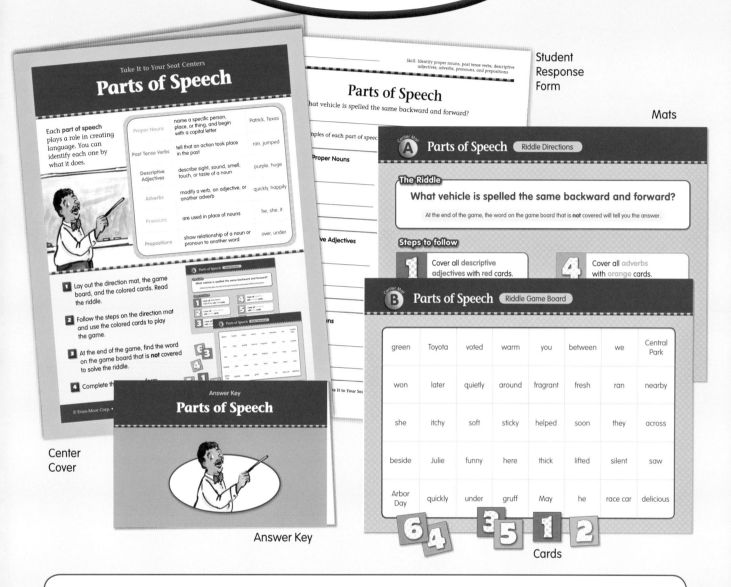

Center Cover

Student Response Form

Mats

Answer Key

Cards

Skill
Identify proper nouns, past tense verbs, descriptive adjectives, adverbs, pronouns, and prepositions

Prepare the Center
Follow the directions on page 3.

Introduce the Center
Demonstrate how to use the center. State the goal: *You will identify words on a game board by their part of speech and cover all but one word to solve a riddle.*

Parts of Speech

Riddle: What vehicle is spelled the same backward and forward?

_____

Write two examples of each part of speech from the riddle cover-up game.

Proper Nouns

_____

_____

Past Tense Verbs

_____

_____

Descriptive Adjectives

_____

_____

Adverbs

_____

_____

Pronouns

_____

_____

Prepositions

_____

_____

Parts of Speech

Each **part of speech** plays a role in creating language. You can identify each one by what it does.

Proper Nouns	name a specific person, place, or thing, and begin with a capital letter	Patrick, Texas
Past Tense Verbs	tell that an action took place in the past	ran, jumped
Descriptive Adjectives	describe sight, sound, smell, touch, or taste of a noun	purple, huge
Adverbs	modify a verb, an adjective, or another adverb	quickly, happily
Pronouns	are used in place of nouns	he, she, it
Prepositions	show relationship of a noun or pronoun to another word	over, under

1 Lay out the direction mat, the game board, and the colored cards. Read the riddle.

2 Follow the steps on the direction mat and use the colored cards to play the game.

3 At the end of the game, find the word on the game board that is **not** covered to solve the riddle.

4 Complete the response form.

Parts of Speech

Riddle: What vehicle is spelled the same backward and forward?

race car
_____

Write two examples of each part of speech from the riddle cover-up game. Examples may vary.

Proper Nouns	Past Tense Verbs
Toyota	voted lifted
Central Park	won saw
Julie	ran
Arbor Day	helped
May	

Descriptive Adjectives	Adverbs
green sticky	later
warm funny	quietly
fragrant thick	nearby
fresh silent	soon
itchy gruff	here
soft delicious	quickly

Pronouns	Prepositions
you we	between
she they	around
he	across
	beside under

Response Form

(fold)

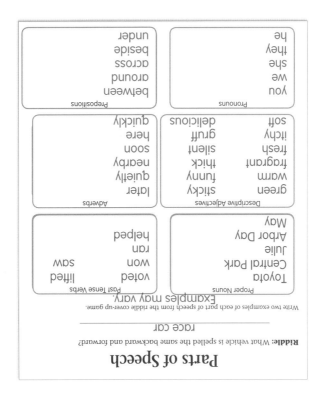

Answer Key

Parts of Speech

Parts of Speech

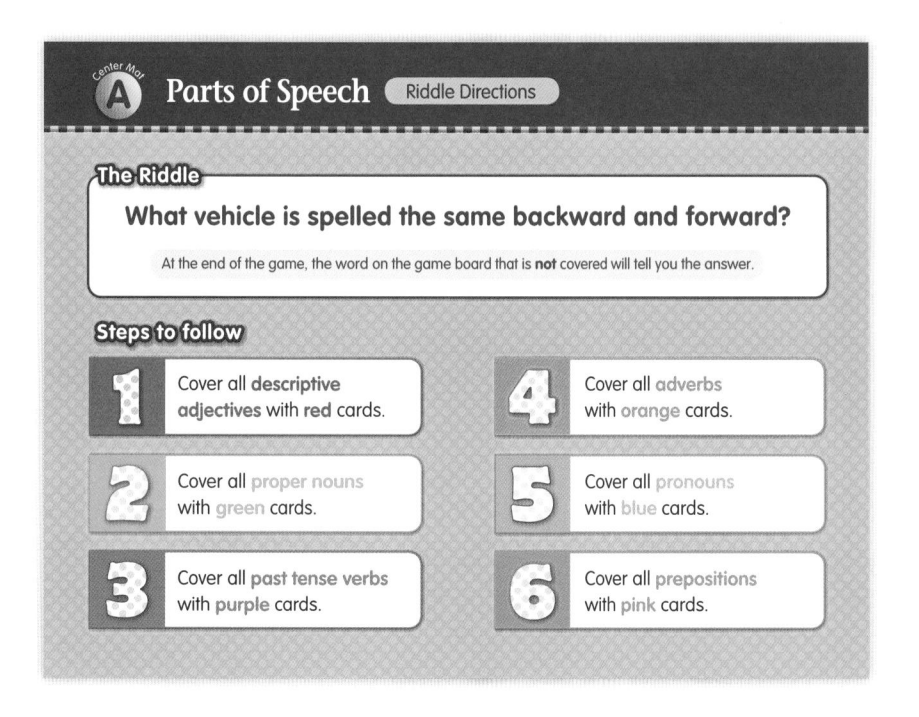

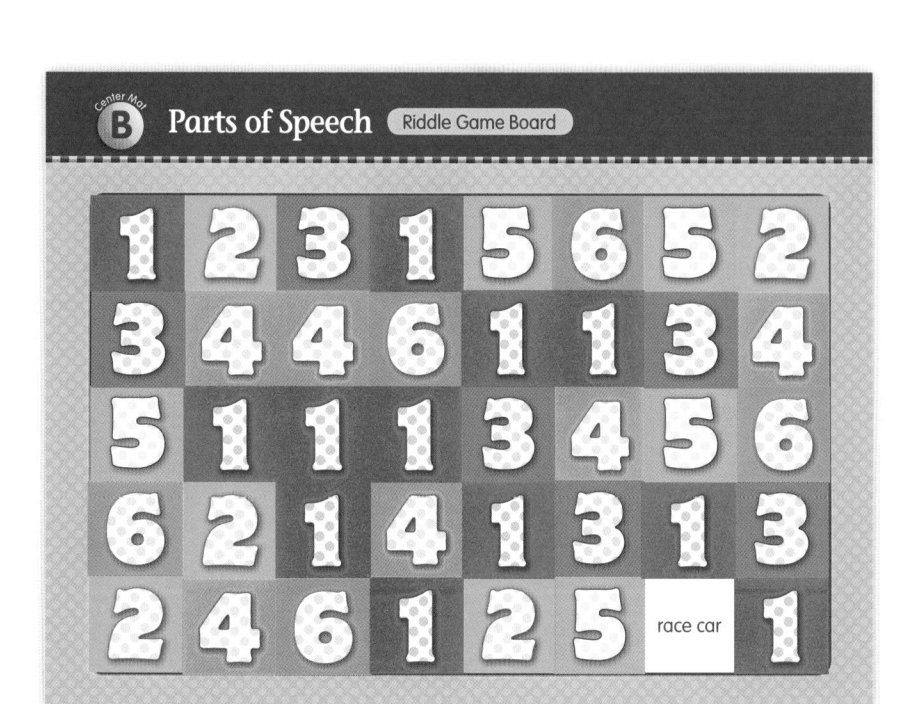

Parts of Speech

The Riddle

What vehicle is spelled the same backward and forward?

At the end of the game, the word on the game board that is **not** covered will tell you the answer.

Steps to follow

 Cover all descriptive adjectives with red cards.

 Cover all proper nouns with green cards.

 Cover all past tense verbs with purple cards.

 Cover all adverbs with orange cards.

 Cover all pronouns with blue cards.

 Cover all prepositions with pink cards.

green	Toyota	voted	warm	you	between	we	Central Park
won	later	quietly	around	fragrant	fresh	ran	nearby
she	itchy	soft	sticky	helped	soon	they	across
beside	Julie	funny	here	thick	lifted	silent	saw
Arbor Day	quickly	under	gruff	May	he	race car	delicious

Take It to Your Seat Centers—Reading & Language • EMC 2845 • © Evan-Moor Corp.

1 1 1 1 1 1
1 1 1 1 1 1
2 2 2 2 2 3
3 3 3 3 3 4
4 4 4 5 5 5
5 5 6 6 6 6
6 6 6

Parts of Speech

Take It to Your Seat
Centers
Reading & Language
EMC 2845
© Evan-Moor Corp.

Parts of Speech

Take It to Your Seat
Centers
Reading & Language
EMC 2845
© Evan-Moor Corp.

Parts of Speech

Take It to Your Seat
Centers
Reading & Language
EMC 2845
© Evan-Moor Corp.

Parts of Speech

Take It to Your Seat
Centers
Reading & Language
EMC 2845
© Evan-Moor Corp.

Parts of Speech

Take It to Your Seat
Centers
Reading & Language
EMC 2845
© Evan-Moor Corp.

Parts of Speech

Take It to Your Seat
Centers
Reading & Language
EMC 2845
© Evan-Moor Corp.

Parts of Speech

Take It to Your Seat
Centers
Reading & Language
EMC 2845
© Evan-Moor Corp.

Parts of Speech

Take It to Your Seat
Centers
Reading & Language
EMC 2845
© Evan-Moor Corp.

Parts of Speech

Take It to Your Seat
Centers
Reading & Language
EMC 2845
© Evan-Moor Corp.

Parts of Speech

Take It to Your Seat
Centers
Reading & Language
EMC 2845
© Evan-Moor Corp.

Parts of Speech

Take It to Your Seat
Centers
Reading & Language
EMC 2845
© Evan-Moor Corp.

Parts of Speech

Take It to Your Seat
Centers
Reading & Language
EMC 2845
© Evan-Moor Corp.

Parts of Speech

Take It to Your Seat
Centers
Reading & Language
EMC 2845
© Evan-Moor Corp.

Parts of Speech

Take It to Your Seat
Centers
Reading & Language
EMC 2845
© Evan-Moor Corp.

Parts of Speech

Take It to Your Seat
Centers
Reading & Language
EMC 2845
© Evan-Moor Corp.

Parts of Speech

Take It to Your Seat
Centers
Reading & Language
EMC 2845
© Evan-Moor Corp.

Parts of Speech

Take It to Your Seat
Centers
Reading & Language
EMC 2845
© Evan-Moor Corp.

Parts of Speech

Take It to Your Seat
Centers
Reading & Language
EMC 2845
© Evan-Moor Corp.

Parts of Speech

Take It to Your Seat
Centers
Reading & Language
EMC 2845
© Evan-Moor Corp.

Parts of Speech

Take It to Your Seat
Centers
Reading & Language
EMC 2845
© Evan-Moor Corp.

Parts of Speech

Take It to Your Seat
Centers
Reading & Language
EMC 2845
© Evan-Moor Corp.

Parts of Speech

Take It to Your Seat
Centers
Reading & Language
EMC 2845
© Evan-Moor Corp.

Parts of Speech

Take It to Your Seat
Centers
Reading & Language
EMC 2845
© Evan-Moor Corp.

Parts of Speech

Take It to Your Seat
Centers
Reading & Language
EMC 2845
© Evan-Moor Corp.

Parts of Speech

Take It to Your Seat
Centers
Reading & Language
EMC 2845
© Evan-Moor Corp.

Parts of Speech

Take It to Your Seat
Centers
Reading & Language
EMC 2845
© Evan-Moor Corp.

Parts of Speech

Take It to Your Seat
Centers
Reading & Language
EMC 2845
© Evan-Moor Corp.

Parts of Speech

Take It to Your Seat
Centers
Reading & Language
EMC 2845
© Evan-Moor Corp.

Parts of Speech

Take It to Your Seat
Centers
Reading & Language
EMC 2845
© Evan-Moor Corp.

Parts of Speech

Take It to Your Seat
Centers
Reading & Language
EMC 2845
© Evan-Moor Corp.

Parts of Speech

Take It to Your Seat
Centers
Reading & Language
EMC 2845
© Evan-Moor Corp.

Parts of Speech

Take It to Your Seat
Centers
Reading & Language
EMC 2845
© Evan-Moor Corp.

Parts of Speech

Take It to Your Seat
Centers
Reading & Language
EMC 2845
© Evan-Moor Corp.

Parts of Speech

Take It to Your Seat
Centers
Reading & Language
EMC 2845
© Evan-Moor Corp.

Parts of Speech

Take It to Your Seat
Centers
Reading & Language
EMC 2845
© Evan-Moor Corp.

Parts of Speech

Take It to Your Seat
Centers
Reading & Language
EMC 2845
© Evan-Moor Corp.

Parts of Speech

Take It to Your Seat
Centers
Reading & Language
EMC 2845
© Evan-Moor Corp.

Parts of Speech

Take It to Your Seat
Centers
Reading & Language
EMC 2845
© Evan-Moor Corp.

Parts of Speech

Take It to Your Seat
Centers
Reading & Language
EMC 2845
© Evan-Moor Corp.

Take It to Your Seat Centers

Analogies

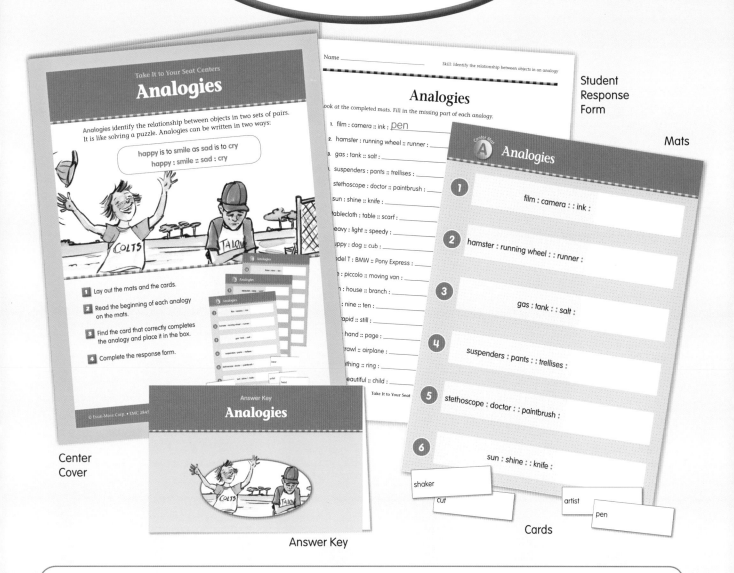

Center Cover

Answer Key

Student Response Form

Mats

Cards

Skill
Identify the relationship between objects in an analogy

Prepare the Center
Follow the directions on page 3.

Introduce the Center
Demonstrate how to use the center. State the goal: *You will read the first part of each analogy and place the card that completes the analogy next to it on the mat.*

Analogies

Look at the completed mats. Fill in the missing part of each analogy.

1. film : camera :: ink : <u>pen</u> _____

2. hamster : running wheel :: runner : _____

3. gas : tank :: salt : _____

4. suspenders : pants :: trellises : _____

5. stethoscope : doctor :: paintbrush : _____

6. sun : shine :: knife : _____

7. tablecloth : table :: scarf : _____

8. heavy : light :: speedy : _____

9. puppy : dog :: cub : _____

10. Model T : BMW :: Pony Express : _____

11. flute : piccolo :: moving van : _____

12. room : house :: branch : _____

13. three : nine :: ten : _____

14. fast : rapid :: still : _____

15. finger : hand :: page : _____

16. baby : crawl :: airplane : _____

17. shirt : clothing :: ring : _____

18. flower : beautiful :: child : _____

Take It to Your Seat Centers—Reading & Language • EMC 2845 • © Evan-Moor Corp.

Analogies

Analogies identify the relationship between objects in two sets of pairs. It is like solving a puzzle. Analogies can be written in two ways:

> **happy** is to **smile** as **sad** is to **cry**
>
> **happy : smile :: sad : cry**

1 Lay out the mats and the cards.

2 Read the beginning of each analogy on the mats.

3 Find the card that correctly completes the analogy and place it in the box.

4 Complete the response form.

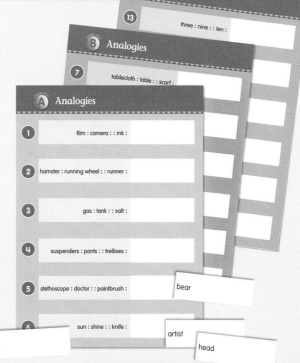

Analogies

13 three : nine : : ten :

B Analogies

7 tablecloth : table : : scarf :

A Analogies

1 film : camera : : ink :

2 hamster : running wheel : : runner :

3 gas : tank : : salt :

4 suspenders : pants : : trellises :

5 stethoscope : doctor : : paintbrush : bear

6 sun : shine : : knife : artist

fly head

Analogies

Look at the completed mats. Fill in the missing part of each analogy.

1. film : camera :: ink : __pen__
2. hamster : running wheel :: runner : __track__
3. gas : tank :: salt : __shaker__
4. suspenders : pants :: trellises : __vines__
5. stethoscope : doctor :: paintbrush : __artist__
6. sun : shine :: knife : __cut__
7. tablecloth : table :: scarf : __head__
8. heavy : light :: speedy : __pokey__
9. puppy : dog :: cub : __bear__
10. Model T : BMW :: Pony Express : __U.S. Postal Service__
11. flute : piccolo :: moving van : __pickup truck__
12. room : house :: branch : __tree__
13. three : nine :: ten : __one hundred__
14. fast : rapid :: still : __calm__
15. finger : hand :: page : __book__
16. baby : crawl :: airplane : __fly__
17. shirt : clothing :: ring : __jewelry__
18. flower : beautiful :: child : __cute__

Response Form

(fold)

Analogies

Answer Key

Answer Key

Analogies

A

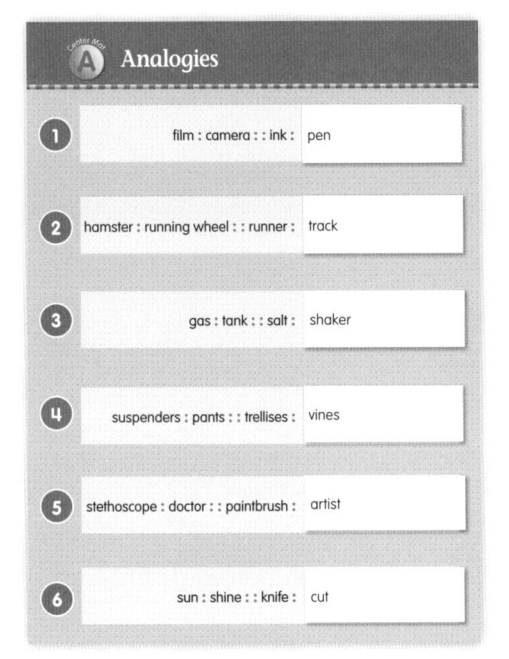

1	film : camera : : ink :	pen
2	hamster : running wheel : : runner :	track
3	gas : tank : : salt :	shaker
4	suspenders : pants : : trellises :	vines
5	stethoscope : doctor : : paintbrush :	artist
6	sun : shine : : knife :	cut

B

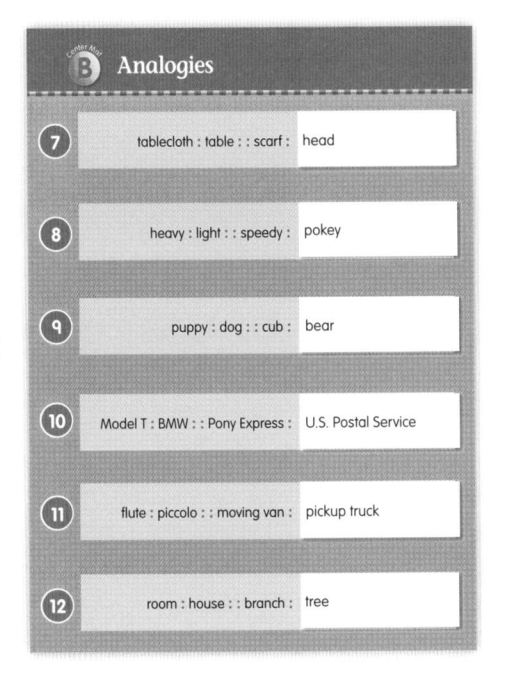

7	tablecloth : table : : scarf :	head
8	heavy : light : : speedy :	pokey
9	puppy : dog : : cub :	bear
10	Model T : BMW : : Pony Express :	U.S. Postal Service
11	flute : piccolo : : moving van :	pickup truck
12	room : house : : branch :	tree

C

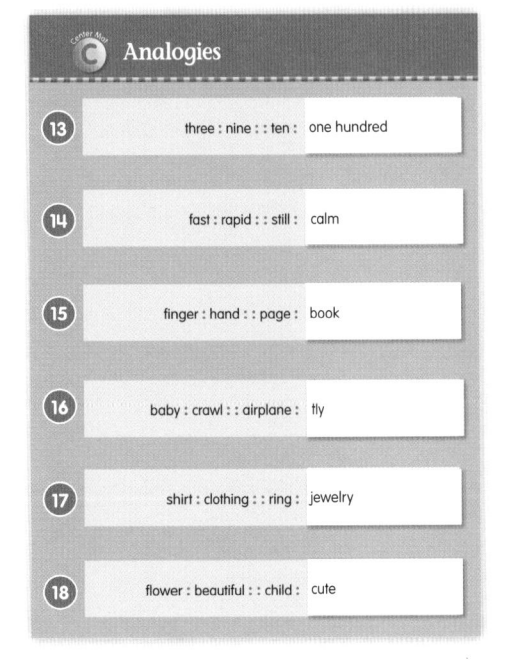

13	three : nine : : ten :	one hundred
14	fast : rapid : : still :	calm
15	finger : hand : : page :	book
16	baby : crawl : : airplane :	fly
17	shirt : clothing : : ring :	jewelry
18	flower : beautiful : : child :	cute

1 film : camera : : ink :

2 hamster : running wheel : : runner :

3 gas : tank : : salt :

4 suspenders : pants : : trellises :

5 stethoscope : doctor : : paintbrush :

6 sun : shine : : knife :

7   tablecloth : table : : scarf :

8   heavy : light : : speedy :

9   puppy : dog : : cub :

10   Model T : BMW : : Pony Express :

11   flute : piccolo : : moving van :

12   room : house : : branch :

13 three : nine : : ten :

14 fast : rapid : : still :

15 finger : hand : : page :

16 baby : crawl : : airplane :

17 shirt : clothing : : ring :

18 flower : beautiful : : child :

pen	track
shaker	vines
artist	head
pokey	bear
U.S. Postal Service	pickup truck
one hundred	calm
book	fly
jewelry	cute
cut	tree

Analogies

Take It to Your Seat Centers—Reading & Language
EMC 2845 • © Evan-Moor Corp.

Analogies

Take It to Your Seat Centers—Reading & Language
EMC 2845 • © Evan-Moor Corp.

Analogies

Take It to Your Seat Centers—Reading & Language
EMC 2845 • © Evan-Moor Corp.

Analogies

Take It to Your Seat Centers—Reading & Language
EMC 2845 • © Evan-Moor Corp.

Analogies

Take It to Your Seat Centers—Reading & Language
EMC 2845 • © Evan-Moor Corp.

Analogies

Take It to Your Seat Centers—Reading & Language
EMC 2845 • © Evan-Moor Corp.

Analogies

Take It to Your Seat Centers—Reading & Language
EMC 2845 • © Evan-Moor Corp.

Analogies

Take It to Your Seat Centers—Reading & Language
EMC 2845 • © Evan-Moor Corp.

Analogies

Take It to Your Seat Centers—Reading & Language
EMC 2845 • © Evan-Moor Corp.

Analogies

Take It to Your Seat Centers—Reading & Language
EMC 2845 • © Evan-Moor Corp.

Analogies

Take It to Your Seat Centers—Reading & Language
EMC 2845 • © Evan-Moor Corp.

Analogies

Take It to Your Seat Centers—Reading & Language
EMC 2845 • © Evan-Moor Corp.

Analogies

Take It to Your Seat Centers—Reading & Language
EMC 2845 • © Evan-Moor Corp.

Analogies

Take It to Your Seat Centers—Reading & Language
EMC 2845 • © Evan-Moor Corp.

Analogies

Take It to Your Seat Centers—Reading & Language
EMC 2845 • © Evan-Moor Corp.

Analogies

Take It to Your Seat Centers—Reading & Language
EMC 2845 • © Evan-Moor Corp.

Fact or Opinion?

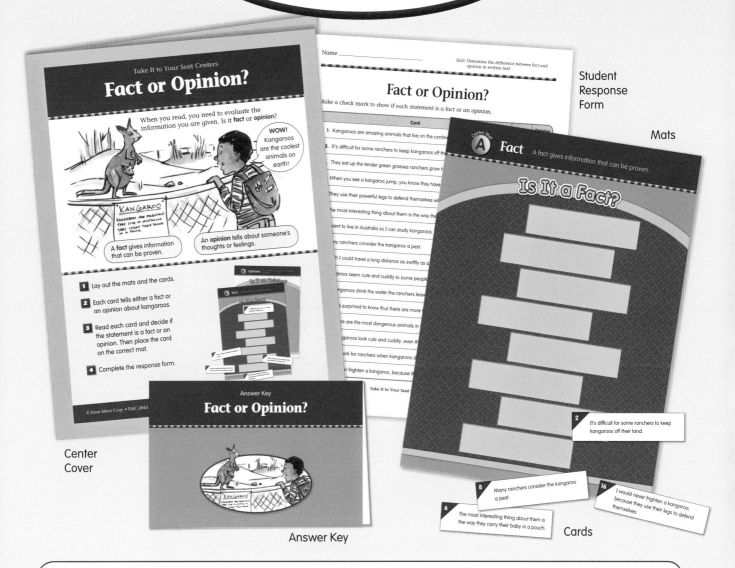

Student Response Form

Mats

Center Cover

Answer Key

Cards

Skill
Determine the difference between fact and opinion in written text

Prepare the Center
Follow the directions on page 3.

Introduce the Center
Demonstrate how to use the center. State the goal: *You will decide which sentence cards about kangaroos are facts and which are opinions.*

Fact or Opinion?

Make a check mark to show if each statement is a fact or an opinion.

Card	Fact	Opinion
1. Kangaroos are amazing animals that live on the continent of Australia.		✔
2. It's difficult for some ranchers to keep kangaroos off their land.		
3. They eat up the tender green grasses ranchers grow to feed the sheep.		
4. When you see a kangaroo jump, you know they have powerful legs.		
5. They use their powerful legs to defend themselves when they are frightened.		
6. The most interesting thing about them is the way they carry their baby in a pouch.		
7. I want to live in Australia so I can study kangaroos.		
8. Many ranchers consider the kangaroo a pest.		
9. I wish I could travel a long distance as swiftly as a hopping kangaroo can.		
10. Kangaroos seem cute and cuddly to some people, but they are wild animals.		
11. The kangaroos drink the water the ranchers leave out for their sheep.		
12. You'd be surprised to know that there are more than 50 types of kangaroos.		
13. Kangaroos are the most dangerous animals in the zoo.		
14. I think kangaroos look cute and cuddly, even though I know they're not.		
15. It's more work for ranchers when kangaroos dig holes and knock down fences.		
16. I would never frighten a kangaroo, because they use their legs to defend themselves.		

Fact or Opinion?

When you read, you need to evaluate the information you are given. Is it **fact** or **opinion**?

WOW! Kangaroos are the coolest animals on earth!

KANGAROO

KANGAROOS ARE MARSUPIALS THEY LIVE IN AUSTRALIA THEY CARRY THEIR YOUNG IN A POUCH.

A **fact** gives information that can be proven.

An **opinion** tells about someone's thoughts or feelings.

1 Lay out the mats and the cards.

2 Each card tells either a fact or an opinion about kangaroos.

3 Read each card and decide if the statement is a fact or an opinion. Then place the card on the correct mat.

4 Complete the response form.

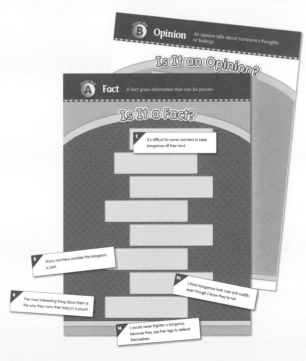

Response Form

Fact or Opinion?

Make a check mark to show if each statement is a fact or an opinion.

Card	Fact	Opinion
1. Kangaroos are amazing animals that live on the continent of Australia.		✓
2. It's difficult for some ranchers to keep kangaroos off their land.	✓	
3. They eat up the tender green grasses ranchers grow to feed the sheep.	✓	
4. When you see a kangaroo jump, you know they have powerful legs.	✓	
5. They use their powerful legs to defend themselves when they are frightened.	✓	
6. The most interesting thing about them is the way they carry their baby in a pouch.		✓
7. I want to live in Australia so I can study kangaroos.		✓
8. Many ranchers consider the kangaroo a pest.	✓	
9. I wish I could travel a long distance as swiftly as a hopping kangaroo can.		✓
10. Kangaroos seem cute and cuddly to some people, but they are wild animals.	✓	
11. The kangaroos drink the water the ranchers leave out for their sheep.	✓	
12. You'd be surprised to know that there are more than 50 types of kangaroos.		✓
13. Kangaroos are the most dangerous animals in the zoo.		✓
14. I think kangaroos look cute and cuddly, even though I know they're not.		✓
15. It's more work for ranchers when kangaroos dig holes and knock down fences.	✓	
16. I would never frighten a kangaroo, because they use their legs to defend themselves.		✓

(fold)

Answer Key

Fact or Opinion?

Answer Key

Fact or Opinion?

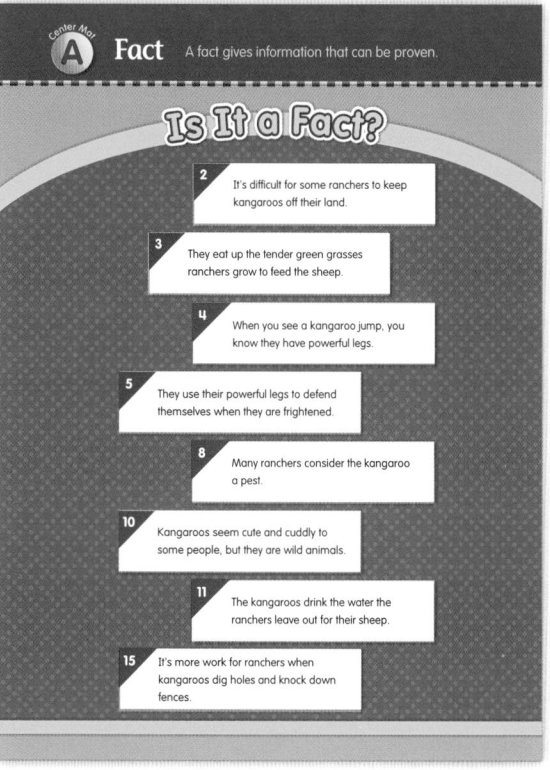

A Fact A fact gives information that can be proven.

Is It a Fact?

2 It's difficult for some ranchers to keep kangaroos off their land.

3 They eat up the tender green grasses ranchers grow to feed the sheep.

4 When you see a kangaroo jump, you know they have powerful legs.

5 They use their powerful legs to defend themselves when they are frightened.

8 Many ranchers consider the kangaroo a pest.

10 Kangaroos seem cute and cuddly to some people, but they are wild animals.

11 The kangaroos drink the water the ranchers leave out for their sheep.

15 It's more work for ranchers when kangaroos dig holes and knock down fences.

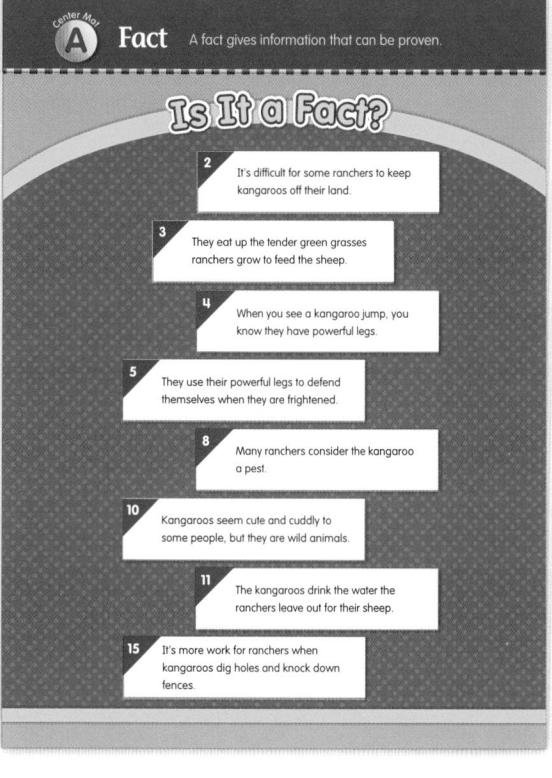

B Opinion An opinion tells about someone's thoughts or feelings.

Is It an Opinion?

1 Kangaroos are amazing animals that live on the continent of Australia.

6 The most interesting thing about them is the way they carry their baby in a pouch.

7 I want to live in Australia so I can study kangaroos.

9 I wish I could travel a long distance as swiftly as a hopping kangaroo can.

12 You'd be surprised to know that there are more than 50 types of kangaroos.

13 Kangaroos are the most dangerous animals in the zoo.

14 I think kangaroos look cute and cuddly, even though I know they're not.

16 I would never frighten a kangaroo, because they use their legs to defend themselves.

Fact

A fact gives information that can be proven.

Is It a Fact?

Is It an Opinion?

Take It to Your Seat Centers—Reading & Language • EMC 2845 • © Evan-Moor Corp.

1 Kangaroos are amazing animals that live on the continent of Australia.

2 It's difficult for some ranchers to keep kangaroos off their land.

3 They eat up the tender green grasses ranchers grow to feed the sheep.

4 When you see a kangaroo jump, you know they have powerful legs.

5 They use their powerful legs to defend themselves when they are frightened.

6 The most interesting thing about them is the way they carry their baby in a pouch.

7 I want to live in Australia so I can study kangaroos.

8 Many ranchers consider the kangaroo a pest.

9 I wish I could travel a long distance as swiftly as a hopping kangaroo can.

10 Kangaroos seem cute and cuddly to some people, but they are wild animals.

11 The kangaroos drink the water the ranchers leave out for their sheep.

12 You'd be surprised to know that there are more than 50 types of kangaroos.

13 Kangaroos are the most dangerous animals in the zoo.

14 I think kangaroos look cute and cuddly, even though I know they're not.

15 It's more work for ranchers when kangaroos dig holes and knock down fences.

16 I would never frighten a kangaroo, because they use their legs to defend themselves.

Fact or Opinion?

Take It to Your Seat Centers—Reading & Language
EMC 2845 • © Evan-Moor Corp.

Fact or Opinion?

Take It to Your Seat Centers—Reading & Language
EMC 2845 • © Evan-Moor Corp.

Fact or Opinion?

Take It to Your Seat Centers—Reading & Language
EMC 2845 • © Evan-Moor Corp.

Fact or Opinion?

Take It to Your Seat Centers—Reading & Language
EMC 2845 • © Evan-Moor Corp.

Fact or Opinion?

Take It to Your Seat Centers—Reading & Language
EMC 2845 • © Evan-Moor Corp.

Fact or Opinion?

Take It to Your Seat Centers—Reading & Language
EMC 2845 • © Evan-Moor Corp.

Fact or Opinion?

Take It to Your Seat Centers—Reading & Language
EMC 2845 • © Evan-Moor Corp.

Fact or Opinion?

Take It to Your Seat Centers—Reading & Language
EMC 2845 • © Evan-Moor Corp.

Fact or Opinion?

Take It to Your Seat Centers—Reading & Language
EMC 2845 • © Evan-Moor Corp.

Fact or Opinion?

Take It to Your Seat Centers—Reading & Language
EMC 2845 • © Evan-Moor Corp.

Fact or Opinion?

Take It to Your Seat Centers—Reading & Language
EMC 2845 • © Evan-Moor Corp.

Fact or Opinion?

Take It to Your Seat Centers—Reading & Language
EMC 2845 • © Evan-Moor Corp.

Fact or Opinion?

Take It to Your Seat Centers—Reading & Language
EMC 2845 • © Evan-Moor Corp.

Fact or Opinion?

Take It to Your Seat Centers—Reading & Language
EMC 2845 • © Evan-Moor Corp.

Fact or Opinion?

Take It to Your Seat Centers—Reading & Language
EMC 2845 • © Evan-Moor Corp.

Fact or Opinion?

Take It to Your Seat Centers—Reading & Language
EMC 2845 • © Evan-Moor Corp.

Word Meaning from Context

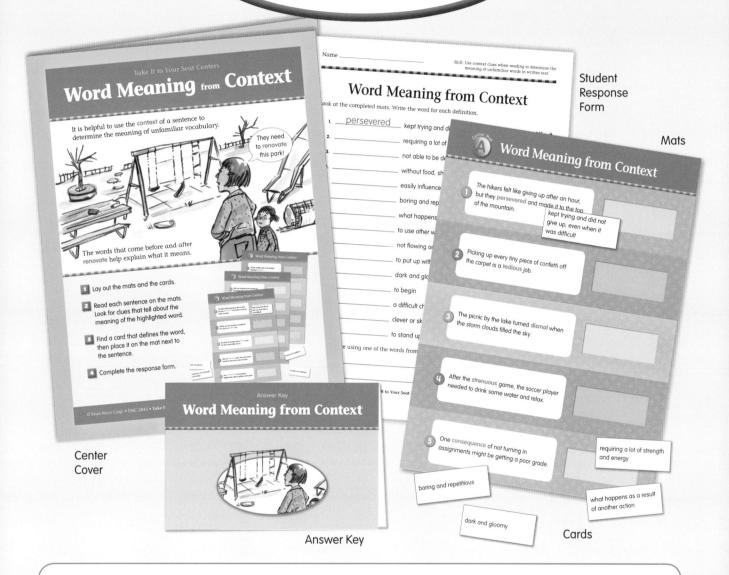

Center Cover

Answer Key

Cards

Student Response Form

Mats

Skill
Use context clues when reading to determine the meaning of unfamiliar words in written text

Prepare the Center
Follow the directions on page 3.

Introduce the Center
Demonstrate how to use the center. State the goal:
You will determine the meaning of an unfamiliar word, using the context of the sentence in which it is used.

Word Meaning from Context

Look at the completed mats. Write the word for each definition.

1. ___persevered___ kept trying and did not give up, even when it was difficult

2. _____ requiring a lot of strength and energy

3. _____ not able to be defeated

4. _____ without food, shelter, or money

5. _____ easily influenced or affected

6. _____ boring and repetitious

7. _____ what happens as a result of another action

8. _____ to use other words to explain something

9. _____ not flowing or moving

10. _____ to put up with something

11. _____ dark and gloomy

12. _____ to begin

13. _____ a difficult choice

14. _____ clever or skillful

15. _____ to stand up against someone or something

Write a sentence using one of the words from above.

_____

_____

Word Meaning from Context

It is helpful to use the **context** of a sentence to determine the meaning of unfamiliar vocabulary.

They need to **renovate** this park!

The words that come before and after **renovate** help explain what it means.

1. Lay out the mats and the cards.

2. Read each sentence on the mats. Look for clues that tell about the meaning of the highlighted word.

3. Find a card that defines the word, then place it on the mat next to the sentence.

4. Complete the response form.

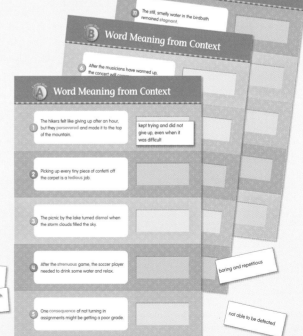

Word Meaning from Context

Look at the completed mats. Write the word for each definition.

1. **persevered** kept trying and did not give up, even when it was difficult
2. **strenuous** requiring a lot of strength and energy
3. **invincible** not able to be defeated
4. **destitute** without food, shelter, or money
5. **susceptible** easily influenced or affected
6. **tedious** boring and repetitious
7. **consequence** at happens as a result of another action
8. **paraphrase** to use other words to explain something
9. **stagnant** not flowing or moving
10. **tolerate** to put up with something
11. **dismal** dark and gloomy
12. **commence** to begin
13. **dilemma** a difficult choice
14. **ingenious** clever or skillful
15. **defiant** to stand up against someone or something

Write a sentence using one of the words from above.

Answers will vary.

_____

(fold)

Word Meaning from Context

Answer Key
Word Meaning from Context

A — Word Meaning from Context

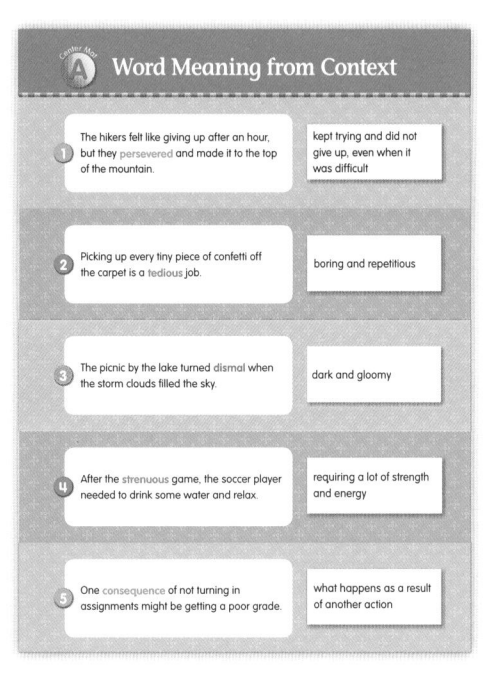

1. The hikers felt like giving up after an hour, but they **persevered** and made it to the top of the mountain. — kept trying and did not give up, even when it was difficult

2. Picking up every tiny piece of confetti off the carpet is a **tedious** job. — boring and repetitious

3. The picnic by the lake turned **dismal** when the storm clouds filled the sky. — dark and gloomy

4. After the **strenuous** game, the soccer player needed to drink some water and relax. — requiring a lot of strength and energy

5. One **consequence** of not turning in assignments might be getting a poor grade. — what happens as a result of another action

B — Word Meaning from Context

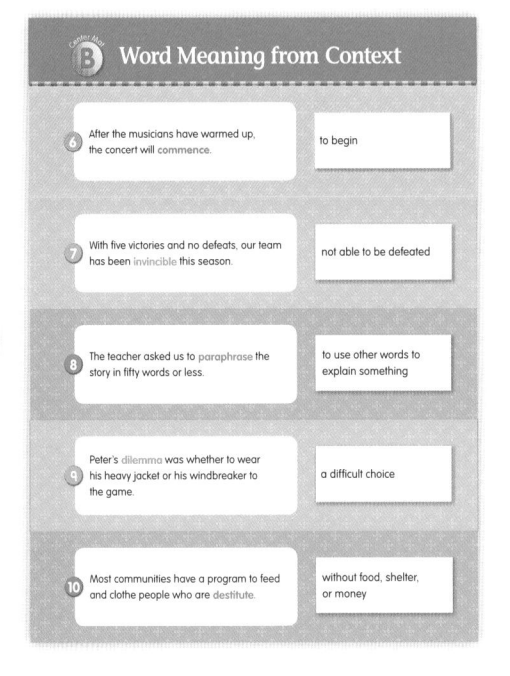

6. After the musicians have warmed up, the concert will **commence**. — to begin

7. With five victories and no defeats, our team has been **invincible** this season. — not able to be defeated

8. The teacher asked us to **paraphrase** the story in fifty words or less. — to use other words to explain something

9. Peter's **dilemma** was whether to wear his heavy jacket or his windbreaker to the game. — a difficult choice

10. Most communities have a program to feed and clothe people who are **destitute**. — without food, shelter, or money

C — Word Meaning from Context

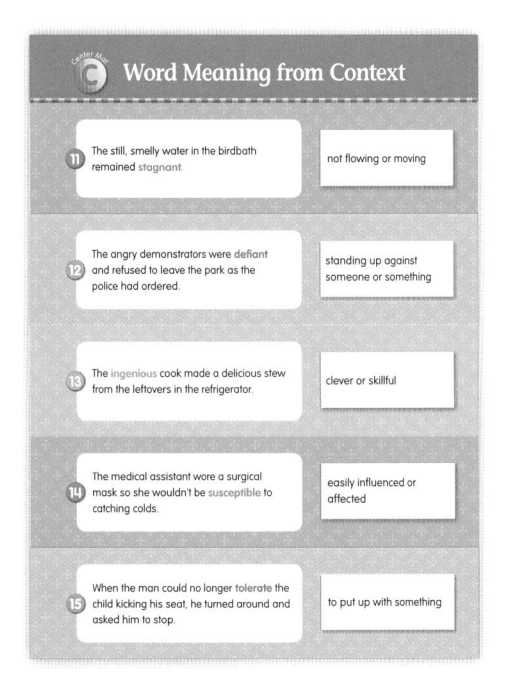

11. The still, smelly water in the birdbath remained **stagnant**. — not flowing or moving

12. The angry demonstrators were **defiant** and refused to leave the park as the police had ordered. — standing up against someone or something

13. The **ingenious** cook made a delicious stew from the leftovers in the refrigerator. — clever or skillful

14. The medical assistant wore a surgical mask so she wouldn't be **susceptible** to catching colds. — easily influenced or affected

15. When the man could no longer **tolerate** the child kicking his seat, he turned around and asked him to stop. — to put up with something

1 The hikers felt like giving up after an hour, but they **persevered** and made it to the top of the mountain.

2 Picking up every tiny piece of confetti off the carpet is a **tedious** job.

3 The picnic by the lake turned **dismal** when the storm clouds filled the sky.

4 After the **strenuous** game, the soccer player needed to drink some water and relax.

5 One **consequence** of not turning in assignments might be getting a poor grade.

Word Meaning from Context

6 After the musicians have warmed up, the concert will **commence**.

7 With five victories and no defeats, our team has been **invincible** this season.

8 The teacher asked us to **paraphrase** the story in fifty words or less.

9 Peter's **dilemma** was whether to wear his heavy jacket or his windbreaker to the game.

10 Most communities have a program to feed and clothe people who are **destitute**.

Center Mat
C

Word Meaning from Context

11 The still, smelly water in the birdbath remained **stagnant**.

12 The angry demonstrators were **defiant** and refused to leave the park as the police had ordered.

13 The **ingenious** cook made a delicious stew from the leftovers in the refrigerator.

14 The medical assistant wore a surgical mask so she wouldn't be **susceptible** to catching colds.

15 When the man could no longer **tolerate** the child kicking his seat, he turned around and asked him to stop.

kept trying and did not give up, even when it was difficult	boring and repetitious	dark and gloomy
requiring a lot of strength and energy	what happens as a result of another action	to begin
not able to be defeated	to use other words to explain something	a difficult choice
without food, shelter, or money	not flowing or moving	clever or skillful
easily influenced or affected	to put up with something	standing up against someone or something

Word Meaning from Context

Take It to Your Seat Centers
Reading & Language
EMC 2845 • © Evan-Moor Corp.

Word Meaning from Context

Take It to Your Seat Centers
Reading & Language
EMC 2845 • © Evan-Moor Corp.

Word Meaning from Context

Take It to Your Seat Centers
Reading & Language
EMC 2845 • © Evan-Moor Corp.

Word Meaning from Context

Take It to Your Seat Centers
Reading & Language
EMC 2845 • © Evan-Moor Corp.

Word Meaning from Context

Take It to Your Seat Centers
Reading & Language
EMC 2845 • © Evan-Moor Corp.

Word Meaning from Context

Take It to Your Seat Centers
Reading & Language
EMC 2845 • © Evan-Moor Corp.

Word Meaning from Context

Take It to Your Seat Centers
Reading & Language
EMC 2845 • © Evan-Moor Corp.

Word Meaning from Context

Take It to Your Seat Centers
Reading & Language
EMC 2845 • © Evan-Moor Corp.

Word Meaning from Context

Take It to Your Seat Centers
Reading & Language
EMC 2845 • © Evan-Moor Corp.

Word Meaning from Context

Take It to Your Seat Centers
Reading & Language
EMC 2845 • © Evan-Moor Corp.

Word Meaning from Context

Take It to Your Seat Centers
Reading & Language
EMC 2845 • © Evan-Moor Corp.

Word Meaning from Context

Take It to Your Seat Centers
Reading & Language
EMC 2845 • © Evan-Moor Corp.

Word Meaning from Context

Take It to Your Seat Centers
Reading & Language
EMC 2845 • © Evan-Moor Corp.

Word Meaning from Context

Take It to Your Seat Centers
Reading & Language
EMC 2845 • © Evan-Moor Corp.

Word Meaning from Context

Take It to Your Seat Centers
Reading & Language
EMC 2845 • © Evan-Moor Corp.

Take It to Your Seat Centers

Main Idea

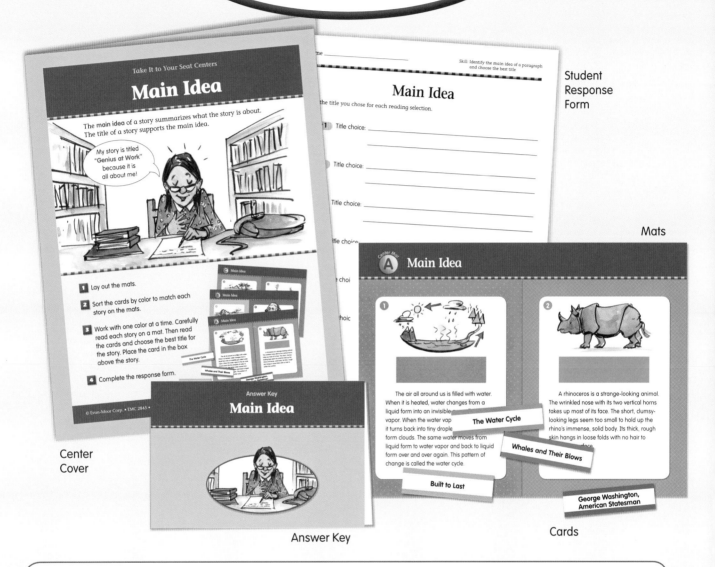

Student Response Form

Mats

Center Cover

Answer Key

Cards

Skill
Identify the main idea of a paragraph and choose the best title

Prepare the Center
Follow the directions on page 3.

Introduce the Center
Demonstrate how to use the center. State the goal: *You will read each selection and choose the best title to reflect the main idea of the story.*

Main Idea

Write the title you chose for each reading selection.

Story 1   Title choice: _____

_____

Story 2   Title choice: _____

_____

Story 3   Title choice: _____

_____

Story 4   Title choice: _____

_____

Story 5   Title choice: _____

_____

Story 6   Title choice: _____

_____

Main Idea

The **main idea** of a story summarizes what the story is about. The title of a story supports the main idea.

My story is titled "**Genius at Work**" because it is all about me!

1 Lay out the mats.

2 Sort the cards by color to match each story on the mats.

3 Work with one color at a time. Carefully read each story on a mat. Then read the cards and choose the best title for the story. Place the card in the box above the story.

4 Complete the response form.

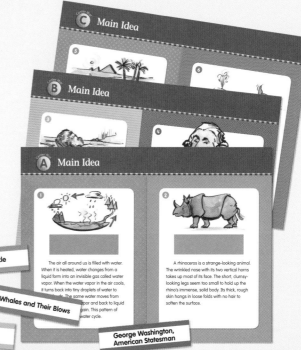

Take It to Your Seat Centers—Reading & Language • EMC 2845 • © Evan-Moor Corp.

Main Idea

Write the title you chose for each reading selection.

Story 1 Title choice: The Water Cycle

Story 2 Title choice: A Strange-Looking Creature

Story 3 Title choice: Nature's Engineer

Story 4 Title choice: Statesman and Farmer

Story 5 Title choice: Birthplace of Modern Civilization

Story 6 Title choice: Whales and Their Blows

Response Form

(fold)

Answer Key

Main Idea

A — Main Idea

1. The Water Cycle

The air all around us is filled with water. When it is heated, water changes from a liquid form into an invisible gas called water vapor. When the water vapor in the air cools, it turns back into tiny droplets of water to form clouds. The same water moves from liquid form to water vapor and back to liquid form over and over again. This pattern of change is called the water cycle.

2. A Strange-Looking Creature

A rhinoceros is a strange-looking animal. The wrinkled nose with its two vertical horns takes up most of its face. The short, clumsy-looking legs seem too small to hold up the rhino's immense, solid body. Its thick, rough skin hangs in loose folds with no hair to soften the surface.

B — Main Idea

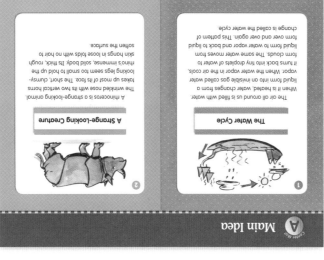

3. Nature's Engineer

The beaver's broad tail acts like a rudder to steer when it swims. Its webbed back feet help it move through the water. Strong front paws help it dig. Two very large orange front teeth gnaw down trees. All in all, the beaver is perfectly equipped to be a pond engineer.

4. Statesman and Farmer

Most people think of George Washington as an important American statesman, the first U.S. president. He was also important in the development of modern farming techniques. At his farm in Virginia, he studied the best way to plant and harvest crops. He experimented with new farming equipment. He even built a special 16-sided barn for threshing the wheat that he grew. He kept meticulous records about each crop and its yield.

C — Main Idea

5. Birthplace of Modern Civilization

The Nile is one of the birthplaces of modern civilization. It is the longest river in the world. The name *Nile* came from the Greek word *neilos*, which means "valley." The water from the river and the fertile soil along its banks made this river valley a good place for ancient peoples to live and farm.

6. Whales and Their Blows

Did you know that whales can be identified by the shape and size of their blows? The blue whale's blow is narrow and high. Right whales make two low blows with their twin blowholes. The humpback whale also has a low blow. The sperm whale makes a blow that is angled forward and to the left. So you can see... it's important to know your blows.

2

A rhinoceros is a strange-looking animal. The wrinkled nose with its two vertical horns takes up most of its face. The short, clumsy-looking legs seem too small to hold up the rhino's immense, solid body. Its thick, rough skin hangs in loose folds with no hair to soften the surface.

1

The air all around us is filled with water. When it is heated, water changes from a liquid form into an invisible gas called water vapor. When the water vapor in the air cools, it turns back into tiny droplets of water to form clouds. The same water moves from liquid form to water vapor and back to liquid form over and over again. This pattern of change is called the water cycle.

Take It to Your Seat Centers—Reading & Language • EMC 2845 • © Evan-Moor Corp.

4

Most people think of George Washington as an important American statesman, the first U.S. president. He was also important in the development of modern farming techniques. At his farm in Virginia, he studied the best way to plant and harvest crops. He experimented with new farming equipment. He even built a special 16-sided barn for threshing the wheat that he grew. He kept meticulous records about each crop and its yield.

3

The beaver's broad tail acts like a rudder to steer when it swims. Its webbed back feet help it move through the water. Strong front paws help it dig. Two very large orange front teeth gnaw down trees. All in all, the beaver is perfectly equipped to be a pond engineer.

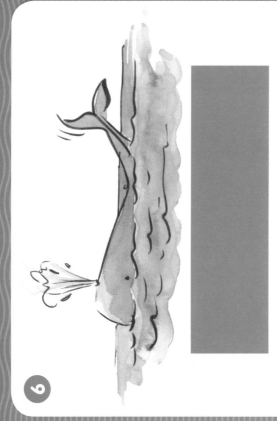

5

The Nile is one of the birthplaces of modern civilization. It is the longest river in the world. The name *Nile* came from the Greek word *neilos*, which means "valley." The water from the river and the fertile soil along its banks made this river valley a good place for ancient peoples to live and farm.

6

Did you know that whales can be identified by the shape and size of their blows? The blue whale's blow is narrow and high. Right whales make two low blows with their twin blowholes. The humpback whale also has a low blow. The sperm whale makes a blow that is angled forward and to the left. So you can see … it's important to know your blows.

A Strange-Looking Creature	Strong Front Paws	Ancient People of the Nile
The Life Cycle of a Rhino	A Busy Beaver	Birthplace of Modern Civilization
Rhinos' Strange Habits	Nature's Engineer	The Longest River
Africa's Biggest and Best	Built to Last	Along the Nile
The Water Cycle	Modern Farming Techniques	All About Whales
Water, Water Everywhere	George Washington, American Statesman	Whales and Their Blows
Changing Weather	Statesman and Farmer	The Size and Shape of Whales
A Cloudy Day	Farming in Virginia	Whale Watching

Main Idea

Take It to Your Seat Centers
Reading & Language
EMC 2845 • © Evan-Moor Corp.

Main Idea

Take It to Your Seat Centers
Reading & Language
EMC 2845 • © Evan-Moor Corp.

Main Idea

Take It to Your Seat Centers
Reading & Language
EMC 2845 • © Evan-Moor Corp.

Main Idea

Take It to Your Seat Centers
Reading & Language
EMC 2845 • © Evan-Moor Corp.

Main Idea

Take It to Your Seat Centers
Reading & Language
EMC 2845 • © Evan-Moor Corp.

Main Idea

Take It to Your Seat Centers
Reading & Language
EMC 2845 • © Evan-Moor Corp.

Main Idea

Take It to Your Seat Centers
Reading & Language
EMC 2845 • © Evan-Moor Corp.

Main Idea

Take It to Your Seat Centers
Reading & Language
EMC 2845 • © Evan-Moor Corp.

Main Idea

Take It to Your Seat Centers
Reading & Language
EMC 2845 • © Evan-Moor Corp.

Main Idea

Take It to Your Seat Centers
Reading & Language
EMC 2845 • © Evan-Moor Corp.

Main Idea

Take It to Your Seat Centers
Reading & Language
EMC 2845 • © Evan-Moor Corp.

Main Idea

Take It to Your Seat Centers
Reading & Language
EMC 2845 • © Evan-Moor Corp.

Main Idea

Take It to Your Seat Centers
Reading & Language
EMC 2845 • © Evan-Moor Corp.

Main Idea

Take It to Your Seat Centers
Reading & Language
EMC 2845 • © Evan-Moor Corp.

Main Idea

Take It to Your Seat Centers
Reading & Language
EMC 2845 • © Evan-Moor Corp.

Main Idea

Take It to Your Seat Centers
Reading & Language
EMC 2845 • © Evan-Moor Corp.